St John's Primary

The
Middle Leader's
Toolkit

John Samuels

The Middle Leader's Toolkit

Copyright © 2018 John Samuels
All rights reserved.

ISBN: 978-1-9875-8725-8

Book design by Sarah E. Holroyd (http://sleepingcatbooks.com)

Preface
• • •

As a Headteacher, County Advisor and Education Consultant it has been my privilege to work with hundreds of Middle Leaders across the country. I have found that the most successful Middle Leaders develop a toolkit of skills, behaviours and processes that support them in what is a wonderful but demanding job. This book outlines some of those skills, behaviours and processes that I hope will prove useful to you and serves as an induction into the role of Middle Leader.

Contents

• • •

Preface iii
Chapter One: Leadership 1
Chapter Two: Managing Chnage 23
Chapter Three: Developing Others and Yourself 38
Chapter Four: Securing Accountability 50
Chapter Five: Developing Pedagogy and Becoming a Leader of
    Learning 63
Chapter Six: Building and Managing Your Team 80
Chapter Seven: Developing Trust and Motivating Staff 97
Chapter Eight: Networking 101
Chapter Nine: Next steps in Leadership 108
Appendix 1 114

CHAPTER ONE
Leadership
• • •

'Leading people is the opposite of trying to control them'

THE LEADERSHIP PILL, Kenneth H. Blanchard, Marc Muchnick

Why Leadership?

You are a successful and well-respected teacher. Only those that have achieved this will know how difficult this was to do. You are well-respected by colleagues, the children you teach and their parents. Why then would you want to put this all at risk by taking on a leadership role? The answer is actually not difficult to see, because it relates to why you have become a good teacher. You want to have a positive influence on the lives of children. So far this has been limited to the children you teach but when you take on a leadership role you immediately increase the number of children you can have a positive impact on. This is what is driving you to begin to think about leadership.

The good news is that the skills that make you a good teacher also have the potential to make you a good leader. Daniel Goleman, who currently works at Rutgers University, developed the concept of Emotional Intelligence which we will return to later. He also maintains a list of characteristics of good and bad leadership. Every time he goes into an organisation he asks the people working there to come up with their list and he keeps a running summary. The list is shown below:

Good boss qualities	Bad boss qualities
Great listener	Blank wall
Encourager	Doubter
Communicator	Secretive
Courageous	Intimidating
Sense of humour	Bad tempered
Decisive	Self-centred
Takes responsibility	Indecisive
Humble	Blames
Shares authority	Arrogant
	Mistrusts

As you can see immediately, many of these good qualities and behaviours are those that make you a good teacher and so you should set off confidently on your journey to leadership.

Leadership and Management

One of the first things to do is to clarify your ideas about what it is to be a leader. Much has been written about leadership but there are some core beliefs and themes about leadership which seem to recur. These are:

- Leadership is about managing change for improvement.
- Leaders have to articulate a vision of where they want to take their followers or members of their team.
- Leaders empower and develop members of their team.
- Leaders practise accountability.

By contrast, management is about making existing systems and structures as efficient and effective as possible.

You will want to be good at both!

Reflecting on what it is to be a leader is an ongoing internal dialogue for successful leaders and so the sooner you start it the better. Talking to colleagues, reading about leadership, attending training, watching videos of successful leaders, are all important contributions to that dialogue. (See suggested reading list, Appendix 1)

Your reflections on leadership and your experience of working with different leaders will no doubt confirm what you already suspected. There is no one way to be a successful leader! This will mean that you have to give some thought not only to what leadership entails but also what sort of leader you want to be. As a Middle Leader do you want to compete with the other Middle Leaders in order to demonstrate that you are better than they? Alternatively, will you be the sort of leader that puts the team before yourself and is happy to contribute in any way you can to the success of others without having to be seen as the hero? This is actually a key decision for you to make, because it will shape your relationship with your peers.

What will be your relationship with the Headteacher? Those who expect loyalty have to model it so if you expect the Headteacher to be loyal to you, you will need to be loyal. However, how will you deal with others criticising the Head in conversation with you?

The other key relationships you have to reflect on are those that you will establish with the members of your team. Recent research by Alex Pentland at the Massachusetts Institute of Technology has established that really effective teams have high levels of social connectivity. Team members know and understand each other and are helpful and supportive, but at the same time can challenge each other when this helps the team move forward. Social connectedness is the measure of how people come together and interact. At an individual level, social connectedness involves the quality and number of connections one has with other people in a social circle of family, friends, and acquaintances.

Even fairly superficial reflections on leadership inevitably lead you to see the importance of relationships, since now you depend on others in order to achieve things. However, building effective relationships is not always easy, especially as a Middle Leader, and we will subsequently explore strategies to help you achieve this.

All schools have a cultural identity and Middle Leaders have to work within this. However, there is the opportunity to develop cultural aspects of working, within your own team. One particular type of culture has the potential not only to deliver high standards of performance but also to help to address some of the complicated relationship issues we have identified. As a new leader you have the opportunity of developing new approaches and behaviours, and one of the most successful is a 'no excuses culture'.

This is defined by Steve Blank, an entrepreneur and professor at Stanford University, as:

> 'No excuses for failures given, just facts and requests for help
> No excuses for failures accepted, just facts, and offers to help'

Implicit in a 'no excuses culture' is a 'no blame culture'. In my experience the most successful schools that I have worked with have a 'no excuses culture' and leaders within those schools sometimes articulate this explicitly and sometimes just model it. I believe being explicit is always the more effective way.

Of course, articulating a belief is the first step, and in order to be seen as authentic, you will need to model this in your words and actions.

Authenticity

One of the key qualities of successful leaders, often cited by their followers, is that they show integrity in terms of their leadership. Indeed, authenticity lays the foundation for trust and respect. Your integrity as a leader is inextricably linked to your authenticity. If we consider the Authenticity Triangle shown below, we can begin to understand more fully how the concept of integrity applies to Middle Leaders.

Consider the triangle to be made of three sections that can slide over each other like a child's toy. Our authenticity as individuals depends on how closely we can hold the triangle together. We know that if we get dislocation between what we say and what we do we run the risk as leaders of being accused of hypocrisy. We also know that followers watch leaders closely and that if dislocation occurs, as it can so easily do given how busy you are and how easy it is to miss something, it can cause immense damage in terms of how you are perceived by your team and other stakeholders.

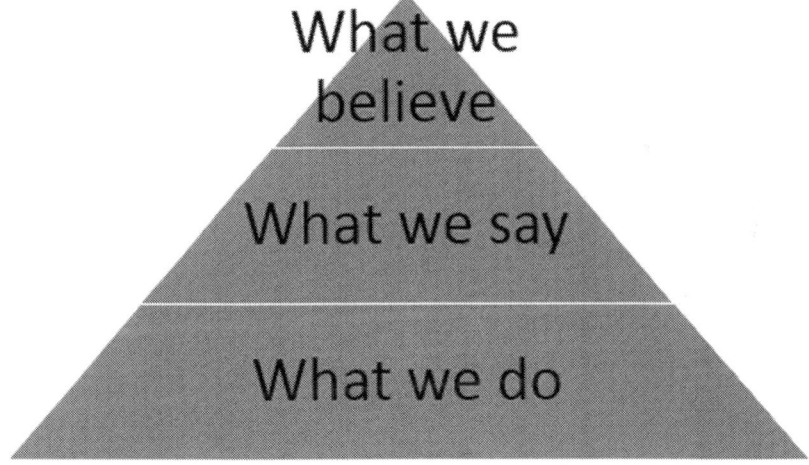

Figure 1. The Authenticity Triangle

Perhaps not so obvious to predict is the dislocation that often occurs between what we believe and what we say. This was brought home to me through my involvement in the selection process for school leaders. I observed that if you ask a number of candidates for their core educational beliefs you usually get very similar answers. My experience, however, would lead me to believe that if each of them was tracked through into their role as leaders, the way in which they acted and led would be completely different. This might have something to do with the context in which they took up the leadership role, but I believe the other reason to be the fact that leaders do not often question and analyse their core beliefs as often as they should and too often add initiatives to their beliefs which they have not thoroughly analysed, questioned and conceptualised. Middle Leaders can be especially prone to this because inevitably they are influenced by what other senior leaders believe. Examples of this would be school leaders who profess to believe in shared leadership but when questioned, find it hard to define precisely what they mean by it. The same can often be true about topics such as independent learning and the creative curriculum. In an interview situation it is not the case that these candidates are trying to deceive, merely that they have not asked themselves the sort of fundamental questions about these developments that would enable them to judge if they believe in them or should reject them. One of those fundamental questions is what would this actually look like in practice and can I describe it? However, if a leader claims shared leadership as a belief, something that, in fact, on deeper analysis they might reject, they can get a dislocation between their stated beliefs and what they articulate and do. Leaders that are prone to this are often accused by their staff of jumping on bandwagons since they are seen to support initiatives that their actions show they really are not committed to.

During your journey to your first leadership role you will have engaged in regular professional development to hone your teaching skills. As a leader you must do the same and model learning for your team. There is a massive body of research on leadership online, as you will find when you begin to interrogate it. Broadly, there are two sorts of contribution to this body of knowledge. There is the work of academics who carry out research about leadership and build conceptual models and then there is the knowledge base of leadership practitioners who work in the field and share their learning.

The power of conversation

One very interesting example of the latter is the work of Susan Scott. Scott maintains an international consulting practice through her firm, Fierce Conversations Inc. She talks about leadership being a series of conversations. Some of these conversations are with individuals, some with groups of people, perhaps your team. These conversations either take you towards where you want to go as a leader or away from it. Sometimes a long way away from it! A symptom of this is how often in your head, often in the evening after work, you go through the conversation you would like to have had rather than the one you actually had.

Susan Scott believes successful leadership is learning how to build relationships in such a way that we can have authentic conversations with each other and avoid this. In trying to turn her beliefs into something practical I have developed a spectrum of conversations that I think school leaders need to be good at. These include:
- Inspiring/motivating conversations
- Conversations which provide direction and advice
- Conversations which move dialogue forward
- Checking conversations
- Conversations that support others by challenging their thinking
- Conversations that unblock
- Courageous conversations that challenge attitudes and behaviours that harm our children's learning

In my experience we tend to be naturally good at some of these types of conversation and not good at others. For example, we tend to be good at giving advice, perhaps too good. This may have something to do with our role as teachers and may be understandable, but it does have unforeseen consequences. If, as a leader, you get into the habit of solving all the problems that your team bring to you by giving them advice, you can become complicit in building a culture of learned helplessness. This is, in fact, quite easy to slip into because you will be so busy that it will sometimes seem like the quick solution. However, if giving people the answer to a problem or issue always worked, you would only need to do it once, and we know this is not the case in reality! If, instead, we support them by asking some good questions which help move their thinking forward, so that they come up with their own solutions, we are helping to grow and develop their leadership qualities. As someone once said, 'people will do their own thinking when you stop doing it for them'. A very important area in which not to over mentor is behaviour management. If you take on trying to solve all the behaviour issues for members of your team, you quickly take on a sort of 'policeman' role. If you are not careful, dealing with these issues becomes the priority rather than improving learning.

Asking good questions is a way of helping your team do new thinking about the issues they face and supporting them in coming up with their own strategies for resolution. The ability to ask good questions is thus a key leadership quality. Here are some examples of good questions leaders might sometimes use:

Questions to provide challenge/support
- What will happen if you do nothing?
- What alternatives could you consider?
- Why do we think this method is the best?
- Do all teachers do it this way?

- Why do other teachers choose a different method?
- Have we any evidence to support this choice?
- What are the downsides of this decision?
- What will we gain by doing this?
- Are the gains we are going to get worth the effort in terms of staff time?
- If we do this how will we know it has been successful?
- What are the implications for our time if we do this?
- How does this fit in with our strategic objectives?
- How will this impact on learning?
- Which group has performed best (gender, ability, ethnicity) and which has performed less well? Why do we think this has happened?
- Which teacher has achieved the best results and why is this?
- What are your next steps?
- How will you know if this is working?
- Which child do you think learnt most and why?
- What would great look like?
- What would you like to be able to say?
- What would you need to do differently?

'Finding out' questions
- Tell me about….
- What happened? What happened next?
- Can you describe it?
- When and where?
- What do you think their motive was?
- What assumptions have you made?
- How did you feel when this happened?
- If they were here talking to me what do you think they would say about what has happened?
- What are your options?

- When you imagine this all going wrong what do you imagine happening?

Questions that connect to previous experience
- Can you think of anything similar from previous experience?
- What did it remind you of?
- How does that compare with what……wrote on the issue?
- What do you think led up to this?
- Are there any general principles you can draw from that?
- What do you think is the worst thing that can happen?

When asking a good question, it is important to give the person time to think and answer it, even if this means there is a period of silence. We sometimes find silence uncomfortable and drive into it but in doing so we often lose the value of the question.

Developing good listening skills.

The other key component of a useful conversation is the ability to listen carefully to another person. This is not only important in helping our understanding of what they are trying to tell us but is an important part in establishing empathy. However, good listening is much easier said than done. It starts by not interrupting people even if they are saying something you disagree with and playing back what you have heard to show that you have listened. This is also useful in building trust. Leaders often have poor listening skills because they listen for influence which is defined as:
- Your view, your judgement.
- Your similar experiences, one-upmanship.
- What does this mean for me?
- What do I need to say next to look good or interested?
- How can I get over my point of view?

Sometimes this type of listening can be useful, when perhaps we want to move a conversation in a particular direction. However, as leaders, there are many times when we need to exhibit more developed listening skills.

If you judge that your listening skills are poor, one way to improve them is to have some 20:80 conversations. These are conversations where you try to limit what you contribute to the conversation to about 20% of the talking and let the other person talk for the other 80% of the time. This is a really good way of helping you focus on managing your talk to listening ratio and listening at an appropriate level!

We will return to some other types of conversation outlined in the spectrum in future chapters.

Earlier I referred to the fact that there are two fields of literature on leadership. I believe Susan Scott illustrates some of the best thinking by a practitioner although there are many others, represented in the reading list at the end of the book, that are worthy of your attention. I want now to look at some of the more recent academic work on leadership. Without doubt Daniel Goleman has had an enormous impact on the way we think about leadership. As mentioned before he is best known for his work on Emotional Intelligence. Goleman showed that successful people, across a wide range of different contexts, tend to have a whole basket of skills and behaviours such as self-awareness, empathy and resilience, which he termed Emotional Intelligence (EI).

In terms of leadership Goleman (2004) identifies six aspects of what he calls Emotionally Intelligent Leadership. These are:

Visionary, sometimes described as Authoritative. Here leaders are articulating in detail what they want to achieve in the future and how the team will work differently in order to achieve this future.

Coaching. Here leaders are working with team members to come up with their own solutions to issues.

Affiliative. Here leaders promote harmony among followers and resolve conflicts.

Democratic. Here the leader lets the group or team participate in decision making.

Pacesetting. Here the leader wants to do things faster and better than others.

Commanding. Here leaders are extremely assertive and want things their way.

All leaders use elements of each of these styles, and each has its value in particular circumstances. For example, if you inherit a team which is badly under-performing, and you need to do something quickly, then a Commanding style of leadership might be very successful. In other circumstances it may not. The most interesting aspects of Goleman's work, however, are where he looks at the results of using these different leadership styles on the organisation and your team. This part of the research was carried out by the Hay Group which is a is a global management consulting firm. In summary the results show

> when a leader is working with staff in Visionary and Coaching mode he or she is building leadership capacity within the organisation and helping to develop other leaders. These modes of EI leadership also have a positive influence on organisational climate.

Pacesetting and Commanding do not build capacity and can have a negative impact on organisational climate. This is interesting in view of the amount of Pacesetting that some leaders engineer. Goleman talks about using Pacesetting 'sparingly'. It is not that any of these styles are wrong, merely that it is useful to consider and take into account the results of using them. Perhaps the most interesting aspect of the impact of the different styles is the effect on standards. Coaching and Visionary are the leadership styles that have the most positive effect on standards. Visionary and Affiliative have the biggest positive effect on commitment to the organisation and Visionary and Coaching have the biggest impact on clarity of purpose.

Developing your coaching skills

This research re-enforces the importance of leaders developing their coaching skills. The skills involved in coaching are focussed on good questioning and active listening as well as the ability to develop empathy and be open minded. The process is intrinsically more challenging than mentoring and offers the opportunity for personal growth for the person being supported. However, coaching is counter-intuitive for some leaders and you may need to work to develop these skills.

When most of us face a problem the process we go through in looking for a solution is to consider similar problems we have had, think about what we did and what resulted, and then decide what to do.

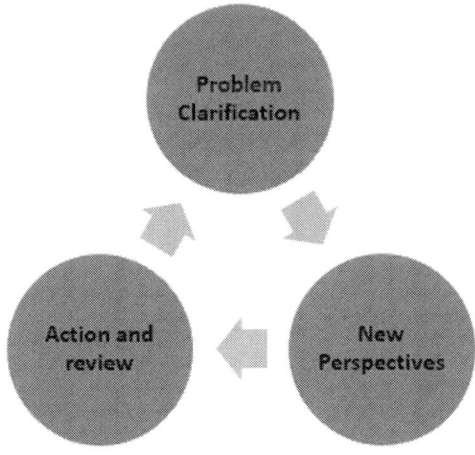

Figure 2. Coaching model

All these processes are based in the past and are very limiting. What a coach does is to try and help the person see new opportunities by getting them to look at the problem from different and new perspectives. This is illustrated in the cycle above.

However, there are a number of other coaching models you might want to consider trying. The most widely used in education is probably the GROW model developed by Sir John Whitmore (1984). There are four stages in this model:

G—goal identification
R—current reality
O—opportunities
W—willingness to act.

Typically, in a GROW coaching session, the coach begins by using listening and questioning skills to establish the outcome the person being coached would be happy with. This is essential because if the coach does not do this he or she may well make inaccurate assumptions about the desired outcome based on what they themselves would want in this situation. The coach would then explore the current situation and the opportunities for action. Finally, after the person being coached has chosen the new action they want to pursue, the coach would discuss barriers as well as timescales for the new strategy.

Some leaders find it useful to introduce coaching to staff through a model but there are potential problems. The coaching can become very formulaic and the model assumes that the person being coached will be aware of the goal when they start which is not always the case. The model also assumes that the coaching process is linear. Often these assumptions do not match reality. For example, it will often be the case that the person will, in fact, start with the symptoms of a problem rather than the core issue which they may not have yet identified. In this situation they are not immediately aware of the goal they want to achieve. Having said this, in trying to develop a coaching culture, the model provides a useful starting point.

The focus of coaching does not have to be a problem and staff are sometimes much more willing to engage in coaching activities that do not start with a problem. For example, two colleagues can have a coaching conversation about a recent successful lesson. The job of the one acting as the coach is to listen and ask some insightful questions which will help the teacher take some deeper learning from this successful lesson into their future planning. This is an activity I have used successfully in a number of schools, as a way of initially engaging staff in coaching activities.

When to coach and when to mentor

In terms of effectively supporting staff to build their coaching skills, and indeed develop your own coaching skills, a key issue is to know when to coach and when to mentor where mentoring is defined as giving advice and solutions and coaching is helping others to come up with their own solutions. If we try to mentor when coaching is needed, almost inevitably the mentoring will fail. The following diagram is helpful in establishing when to coach and when to mentor.

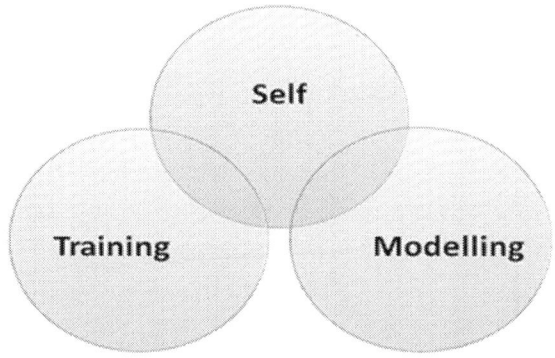

Figure 3. When to coach and when to mentor.

Whenever a person carries out a role, the way in which they carry out the role is influenced by three domains. Firstly, any training they have received which affects the way they carry out the role. Secondly any modelling they have experienced that affects how they carry out the role and thirdly their own personality, life experience and DNA which will also have an effect. This last domain is labelled Self. The relative importance of the three influences varies from one role to another and from one person to another. If you have had a rich training experience this will be a larger domain than it would be for someone who had a poor experience. If we consider the role of somebody working on a supermarket checkout, the training and modelling areas of the model would be very influential. They might receive training perhaps on a dummy checkout and then go on to watch somebody modelling the work on a check-out and both these would have a large influence on how they did the job. Once fully trained and working, however, the Self segment would play quite a small role in how they carried out their job, since social interactions in the role are short, and often perfunctory on a supermarket checkout. If there were problems while working at the check-out usually the person would indicate this to a supervisor, and the supervisor would come to help them and would mentor them by providing a solution. This observation can help us to establish when it is best to mentor and when it is best to coach. Mentoring is the first strategy to try if the problem is perceived to be a matter of lack of training or modelling. However, if the issue is related to the Self segment, for example to do with relationships, then mentoring will often not be appropriate since it would be very difficult to give another person answers in this area where we may have completely different experiences and personalities.

In teaching, the Self component is very large compared to the training and modelling components and therefore the potential for mentoring is much reduced. If you have watched lots of different teachers teach you can see how much of what they do depends on their personality and relationships with children. In my experience, often in schools we have the balance between coaching and mentoring wrong, and too much mentoring can occur or mentoring can go on for too long, without enough coaching to give more balance. Often, therefore, we end up mentoring when we should be coaching. Consider for example two Newly Qualified Teachers (NQTs). One is coping very well but perhaps having a problem with a couple of learners. Usually we would mentor in this case and offer some advice perhaps in terms of classroom management or a more differentiated approach to learning. This would probably work because the issue often lies in the training or modelling area. However, if we had an NQT who was having problems with many of the learners or classes they taught we tend to adopt the same strategy and offer advice. This normally fails, and they come back for help and they are often offered yet more advice. The reason the advice fails is because the problem is much more likely to be tied up with their personality or the way they interact with the learners i.e. in the Self area, and we might be much more effective by coaching them. They could then come up with their own approaches to help tackle the issue. Given the potential power of coaching it is no wonder that Goleman (2004), identifies the coaching leadership style as the one that is most effective in building capacity and improving standards.

Developing the habits of effective Leadership

One of the frustrations of Middle Leadership is that although you will have some power over decision making, ultimately the Headteacher and Senior Leadership Team will make final decisions in many areas. Some Middle Leaders find this very difficult to handle and end up very frustrated. As a Middle Leader I think some advice from Stephen Covey, who was an American educator, from his book 'Seven Habits of Highly Effective People' is useful to keep in mind. He says very effective leaders concentrate on what they have control of. Where they don't have control, but have some influence, they use their influence to bring about the sort of changes and policies they support. However, they spend very little time in the concern zone, worrying about things they have no control over, which leads only to frustration.

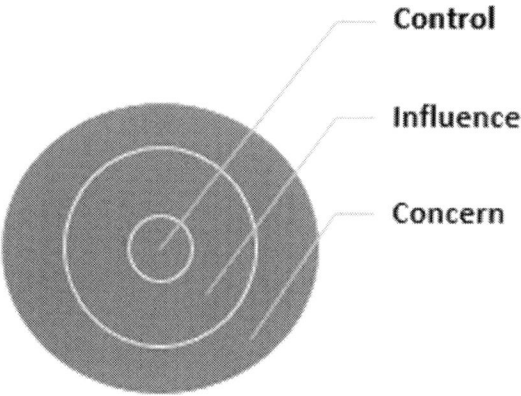

Figure 4. Based on Stephen Covey's book 'Seven Habits of Highly Effective People'

Developing good influencing skills is thus very useful as a Middle leader, and I have found the summary below to be very useful in de-mystifying what those skills would look like in practice.
1. Use reasoned, positive arguments and in a calm way.
2. Use questions to challenge when you disagree with others.
3. Look for common ground and listen to what the other person is saying.
4. Know when to compromise so that both sides take something from the process.

5. Manage tone and pace when you speak and use open body language.

The most successful Middle Leaders are often the ones who are just that little bit more creative in their leadership. This does not mean you have to have all the ideas! The role of a creative leader is not in fact to have all the ideas; it is to create a culture where everyone can have ideas and feel that they're valued. Therefore, this is much more about creating climates. This involves a focus on solutions and opportunities rather than problems, encouraging intellectual curiosity, recognising strengths in others and remembering simple solutions are often preferable to complex ones.

We have already said that your relationships with your team will be critical in terms of your leadership and it is worth just reflecting on the nature of those relationships. These are the people whom you will see and work with most often and inevitably interact with more than other staff. It is important, however, to try and avoid developing favourites. This is easier said than done but I think it is important to be aware that this can be an issue for team members. Avoiding unprofessional conversations about staff is also important and I think it is a good discipline to try and imagine the member of staff present when you are talking to someone about somebody who is not there , and have the conversation accordingly.

Assertiveness

One reason to manage the relationships with the team carefully is that as a Middle Leader you will need to be assertive and sometimes leaders find this difficult if they have become too close to members of the team. Assertiveness lies between submissiveness and aggressiveness. The most effective leaders are neither submissive nor aggressive. Some people are naturally assertive but if does not come naturally to you there are some tips for developing it.

1. Use of the word I. e.g. 'I want you to ……………' Don't use others as the reason. i.e. 'The Head/Ofsted wants/needs you to…..'
2. Let others know when their behaviour has a negative effect on you. 'Because you haven't finished the reports I will not be able to work on them today as I planned'.
3. Make the consequences of not changing a behaviour clear. 'If this continues I will have no option but to…….'
4. Point out any double standards. 'I followed our agreed ……………..but you have not done the same'

It is also important to understand assertive body language and the non-verbal communications we make with our team. Here are some pointers:

- EYE CONTACT – Make sure the person is more interesting than what is on the floor. Look at the person most of the time. But do not stare at people 100 percent of the time (this is an act of aggression!)
- DISTANCE/PHYSICAL CONTACT – Keep a comfortable distance.
- GESTURES – Use hand gestures to add to what you are saying but remember that you are not conducting an orchestra.
- FACIAL EXPRESSIONS – Your face should match your emotion and what you are saying. Don't laugh when you are upset and don't have a frown when you are happy. A relaxed, neutral face is best when you are happy. A relaxed, serious face is best when you are upset.
- VOICE TONE, INFLECTION, VOLUME – When you are giving an assertive message, you want to be heard. Pay attention to the tone of your voice (happy, whiny, upset), the inflection of your voice (emphasis on syllables), and volume of your voice (whisper to yell).

- LISTENING – An important part of assertiveness. If you are making statements that express your feelings (without infringing on the rights of others) you need to give the other person a chance to respond.

Of course, what a person says is one of the most important parts of the assertive message. Plan it carefully, think about what the response might be and how you will then respond.

Critical Thinking.
The last aspect of leadership that I want to look at in this chapter is critical thinking. Good Middle Leaders make more good decisions than bad ones and critical thinking is one method to help ensure that you do this. The Watson-Glaser RED model provides a simple but useful framework for critical thinking. This has now been developed into a test that is often used in recruitment, especially in industry.

RED Model
There are three stages in the model.

Recognise assumptions
Assumptions arise when there are gaps in knowledge. It is deceptively easy to listen and assume that information presented is true even though no evidence was given to back it up. Noticing and questioning assumptions helps to reveal information gaps or unfounded logic. Once you notice assumptions, it can be very helpful to examine the differences in the way people will fill in these gaps.

Evaluate arguments
The art of evaluating arguments entails analysing information objectively and accurately, questioning the quality of supporting

evidence, and understanding how emotion influences the situation. Common barriers include tending to favour information that is in line with a previously held view or allowing emotions to get in the way of objective evaluation.

Draw conclusions
Bringing diverse information together to arrive at conclusions that logically follow from the available evidence is crucial when making a decision. People who can do this are careful not to inappropriately generalise beyond the evidence and they can change their position when the evidence warrants doing so. They are often characterised as having "good judgment".

This short introduction into the body of knowledge about leadership is intended to kick start the ongoing internal and external dialogue you have about leadership. There are many sources of material to stimulate this dialogue, including key texts, TED talks from great leaders and networking and listening to other colleagues.

Key Points
- Leadership is more about listening and asking good questions than telling people what to do.
- Effective leaders continually reflect on the nature and practice of leadership.

Further reading:
Collins J. (2001) *Good to Great* Published Harper Business. ISBN: 9780066620992
Blanchard K, Johnson S. (1994) *The one minute manager*, Harper Collins. ISBN 10 0006367534

CHAPTER TWO
Managing Change
• • •

'The secret of change is to focus all of your energy not on fighting the old, but on building the new'
Socrates

Middle Leaders often come into the job with a ready-made list of tasks to take on. Before embarking on specific changes, however, it is worth considering the culture within the team you have inherited. Cultural issues - low expectations for example - can manifest themselves in many ways. It would be easy to focus on the symptoms of this, poor data in a particular area for instance, but the problem will only really be tackled by challenging the culture that led to it. Cultural changes involve changing what people think as well as what they do. Although as a Middle Leader you have limited influence on the whole school culture, you can impact on your own team's culture as evidenced by multiple research on 'in-school variation'. This shows that even in schools where standards are low, some teams buck the trend and perform well.

Language plays a very important part in developing cultures and as a leader, you need to be conscious of the effect the language you use has on the culture within the team. For example, if I want high expectations, would I talk about low ability groups or low attaining groups? Low ability implies a global learning problem whereas low attainment, let's say in writing, does not preclude high attainment in music. Similarly, if as a teacher, I have a low ability group it would be very difficult not to let this influence what I thought I could achieve with them. Now that you have become a leader, your team will watch carefully what you say and take meaning from it. You need to ensure they take the meaning you intended. This focus on what you say can be positive but can also have unforeseen consequences!

As a leader, you will be partly judged on your ability to manage change successfully. Managing change successfully will be easier if there are high levels of trust within your team. Trust is related to transparency and clarity and high levels of trust are especially important at times of change. One way of developing this is to develop a toolkit of approaches as a leader which you can share with your team so that they understand both the need for change and the way you are managing it. Some of the tools we are going to discuss using are designed to avoid problems in the planning stage; others are concerned with implementation. I have chosen to share tools which I, and other school leaders, have used successfully but there are many others available which you might also like to a look at. For example, there are many models for managing change such as the Kotter model, which is widely used.

Often Middle Leaders feel the need to bring about improvements quickly. Sometimes the pressure for a solution leads to poor investigation of possible causes and poor planning of solutions. This can lead to a tendency to look for 'the silver bullet' solutions. Very rarely is there just one strategy to address an issue and yet in many Improvement Plans you often see an issue followed by one solution, 'the silver bullet'. The danger is that this can lead to everybody working really hard to solve the wrong problem or what Jim Collins (2001) calls the 'doom loop' i.e. reaction to a problem without real understanding.

Fishbone analysis

The Fishbone analysis is a useful starting point when planning to address a difficult issue and avoiding 'the silver bullet' syndrome.

When you have a serious problem, it's important to explore all of the things that could cause it, before you start to think about a solution. It is also important to use a process that involves and utilises the expertise of all your team. The Fishbone analysis is a tool which helps you to do this. It is very easy to use, and used with a team to encourage their involvement and buy-in to the process of finding a solution.

Steps:

1. Identify the problem or issue you want to look at and this becomes the head of the fishbone.
2. Next explore the causes or contributors to the issue and these become the main fish bones.
3. For each of these main fish bones brainstorm around each "cause" to document those things that contributed to the cause.

A worked example for improving Behaviour for Learning is shown in Figure 5:

The visual representation ensures that all the thinking is captured. If this had just been a team discussion about the issue a lot of the thinking would have been lost as one point was made after another. Also, because this is a visual representation of the team's thinking, it can be stored and revisited if needed to continue the process. Once complete, the team chooses which areas they are going to tackle to resolve the issue. Very rarely would this result in just one approach or 'silver bullet' to solve the problem. Some of the things you can do will be much easier to implement than others.

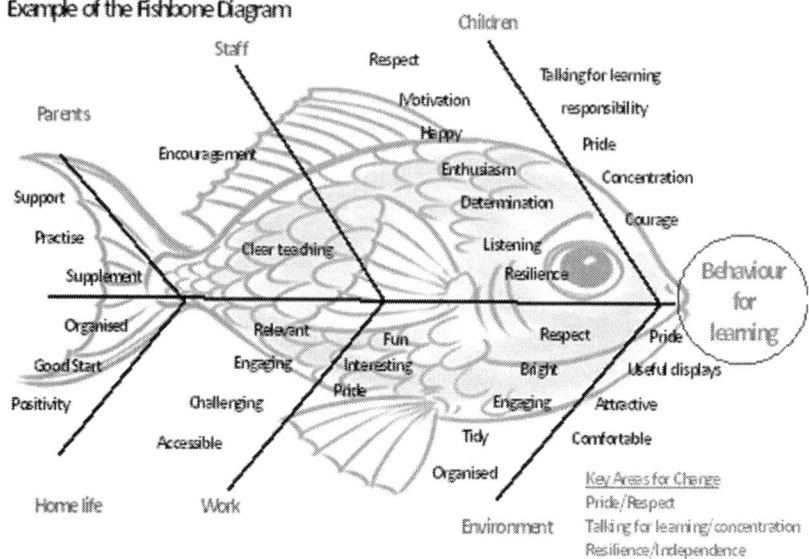

Figure. 5 Fishbone analysis

The Fishbone tool can be used with different groups of staff. For example, if you were looking at Behaviour for Learning, you might do the analysis with several groups—teachers, teaching assistants and children—and look for links. The one illustrated above was completed by Year 6 children facilitated by their teacher. When a number of different groups have carried out the Fishbone you can look for common themes or threads, knowing if you choose to act on one of these, many of the groups involved will buy into the solution.

The Fishbone analysis often results in a number of things you can change relatively easily and a number of things you might change but would require more effort and resource. Deciding which of these to choose to do can be difficult. A tool which can help with this problem is the Force Field analysis.

Force Field analysis

There are many useful tools to help you to manage change but perhaps none more useful than Kurt Lewin's (1951) Force Field analysis. This tool can not only help decide whether a proposed change is worth the effort but also what the potential barriers to the change may be. The analysis is demonstrated in Figure 6. All the positive reasons for carrying out the change are shown on the left-hand side. The relative importance of each aspect of improvement is represented by the length of the line. On the right-hand side are the problems the change will cause or the barriers to change. Again, the relative importance of these is represented by the length of the lines. Once the analysis is finished the length of the lines on each side is compared to indicate the overall gain to be made when the change is implemented. After cancelling out the negatives the longer the remaining gain lines the better the possible outcome when the change is made and the bigger the driver to carry forward the change. Although there is definitely an element of subjectivity to the process it does provide a framework for weighing up the potential gains and downsides of different options and, if used with your team or a group of people, it can become more objective.

There are several other benefits to the analysis. Once the barriers have been identified strategies can be developed to address them. This is important because, if not addressed, some of these barriers may grow and actually prevent the change embedding. Another advantage is that the analysis helps you manage expectations more effectively. By outlining both positives and negatives to your team they have more realistic expectations of the gains the change will bring, and you are not put in a position where you are seen to be 'selling' the change.

A simple worked example is shown below. Suppose you want to introduce a more creative thematic approach to the delivery of the curriculum. You may judge that this will lead to better standards of literacy, learners will be more engaged in their learning and staff will be able to be more creative in the classroom. However, perhaps not all learners will welcome the change. Perhaps some who are doing very well under the present system will not. Also, time and resources will need to be allocated to the change and some staff may not be naturally good at this type of planning and may need training or coaching. If not addressed some of these barriers may grow and cause the change to fail.

The Force Field analysis provides Middle Leaders with a useful cost benefit tool and although you might not apply it for every change you are considering, for those which you are looking to have the biggest impact on standards it is always wise to apply it.

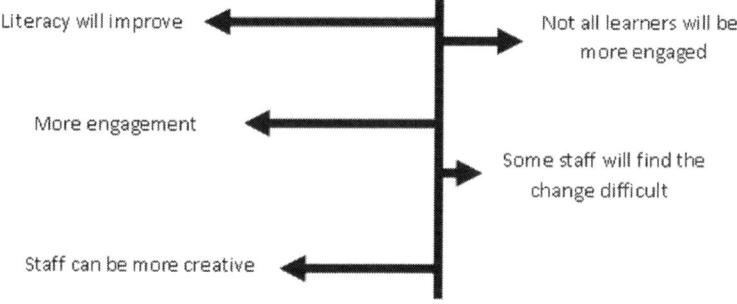

Figure. 6 Force Field analysis

Sometimes Middle Leaders are forced to implement a change that they would not do if the decision was theirs alone. In these circumstances it is especially important to work on reducing barriers since this will improve net gains.

Implementing Change

One of the major reasons that change fails is that implementation times are too short and the barriers to change are underestimated.

This can be caused by new Middle Leaders' understandable desire to make an impression quickly by introducing changes. There is a lot of research on managing the change process, but I think some of the most useful was carried out by Richard Beckhard who was a professor at the Massachusetts Institute of Technology.

Beckhard–Harris Change equation

This is not the only model for managing change but is one of the simplest and most powerful. Adopting a model for change which is shared and understood throughout your team builds transparency and trust. In his research Beckhard showed that in order to overcome the inertia which is associated with change management three things must be in place. He expressed this in the form of an equation:

Need x Vision x First steps > Resistance to change.

Figure. 7 Beckhard Change Equation

Beckhard found that if any of these three factors, Need, Vison or First steps, were not delivered effectively, when managing the change process, then the change would not embed. The first step is to establish the need for the change. In my experience the best way to establish need is to evidence it with as much primary data as you can, in order to avoid relying on opinion, which so easily can turn into a difference of opinion and potential conflict. When he talks of vision, Beckhard is not talking of a strap line but a vivid picture of how this change would affect the work that your team, who will be implementing the change, what they would do on a daily basis. They need to see what the change would mean to them if they are to understand and support it. Sometimes leaders fall into the trap of defining the vision in terms of outcomes rather than inputs, which staff find both unfair and unhelpful. Finally, putting in place some easily achievable first steps will help move the change forward quickly, and reinforce for staff that a change process is occurring. If Middle Leaders embark on change without really establishing Need, then inevitably staff will feel ambivalent at best in terms of the implementation, even when they are provided with first steps. If they are convinced of the need but have no understanding of how the change will affect them in the long term, they will be anxious about embarking on the proposed change and may lack commitment and be unable to exhibit initiative. If they are convinced of the need for change and can see how it could work for them but don't have the first steps to move forward, they cannot effectively begin the change.

Evaluating the progress of the changes you have made

Another reason that changes fail to embed and deliver the gains hoped for, is due to the fact that often we do not track the success of the change effectively as we move through the change process. Learning, which is naturally the focus of the most important changes in school, is complex and we are often looking for improvements in key stage data as way of judging the success of a change in learning strategies. However, the time between introducing a change and seeing the impact on key stage data is rarely short and if we don't monitor how the change is progressing before we have the final data, we often only find out too late that it has not been effective.

Adopting a more functional method of evaluating change can help address this problem. I have used this simple model with a number of Middle Leaders. It is adapted from the Training and Development Agency (TDA) impact evaluation model. This is a four-step model consisting of four stages:

INPUTS—often training sessions, meetings, discussions or dialogues

OUTPUTS— what has changed immediately after the input—often changes in understanding, attitude, confidence or motivation

INTERIM OUTCOMES—often changes in behaviour

LONG TERM OUTCOMES—often changes in data

The last three stages must be rigorously evidenced, in order to track the progress of change.

For example, suppose you want to introduce Assessment for Learning (AfL). One important input might be a team inset day by way of introduction. If we identify explicitly what the outputs are going to be, we will deliver a much more focussed and better day. Suppose we are looking for team members to feel more confident, understand AfL and see opportunities to use it, and we are hoping to see this in action when the next cycle of lesson observations begin the following term. Using the model, we would have to gather evidence the day after the inset to see whether we have achieved our intention in terms of our team feeling more confident etc. This could be done by talking to individual staff or using a questionnaire. Where particular staff haven't reached the level of confidence we want, we might need to provide another input for them until this is achieved. We often miss out this step and find out much later that our input didn't work as well as we hoped. Similarly, when we do the lesson observations, if some staff are not using AfL as intended we need to provide extra inputs. This method of monitoring the implementation of change makes it much more likely it will embed and have the desired effect. It also helps avoid making the mistake of 'declaring victory too quickly' which often occurs in change management.

Checking with staff that inputs have been effective also makes them more accountable for the implementation and delivery of the change. There are many other evaluation models which could be used but again I have chosen a simple one that I know works from my own practice. If a leader uses a model of evaluation, known to all team members, it offers the opportunity of developing a shared leadership language and understanding around a key process in terms of the success of the team. At a time when schools are being urged to become self-improving organisations, a robust approach to evaluation is likely to be even more important in the future. If, as a Middle Leader, you are modelling effective evaluation, this will also influence the way your team work and make them more evaluative.

Change affects people differently

Finally, one of the most perceptive things I have read about why change often fails was in a presentation giving the three most important reasons for failure. These were:
1. People are different
2. People are different
3. People are different

Exaggeration for effect maybe, but so often true. When leaders introduce change they tend to lump staff together as a group in terms of how they plan to introduce it. The impact evaluation model helps to avoid this and there are other frameworks which are useful for this purpose. Such a model, that can be used to take a differential approach to change in terms of the members of your team, is one used by Professor John West Burnham (A Think Piece for NCSL New Visions course). This is the Readiness and Capability tool shown in Figure 8, below. Staff in your team can be placed in one of the four areas in terms of their readiness and capability to introduce a particular change. Those in area 1 are the most capable and most motivated and are potential change agents. Those in area 2 are motivated but may need skilling up. They may need some extra mentoring or coaching in order to be able to carry out the change. Those in area 3 have the capability but not the motivation and your job here is to find what will motivate them. This may involve spending some time finding this out but will be time well spent. Those in area 4 have neither the capability nor motivation and are problematic in that the leader has to decide if the time spent with them will ever make them competent or motivated. If the change embeds with the majority of staff, then making it team policy and dealing with these staff who fail to implement the policy becomes easier and a disciplinary issue.

The Readiness and Capability tool provides a framework to begin to consider staff as individuals with regard to change rather than treating them as a single entity.

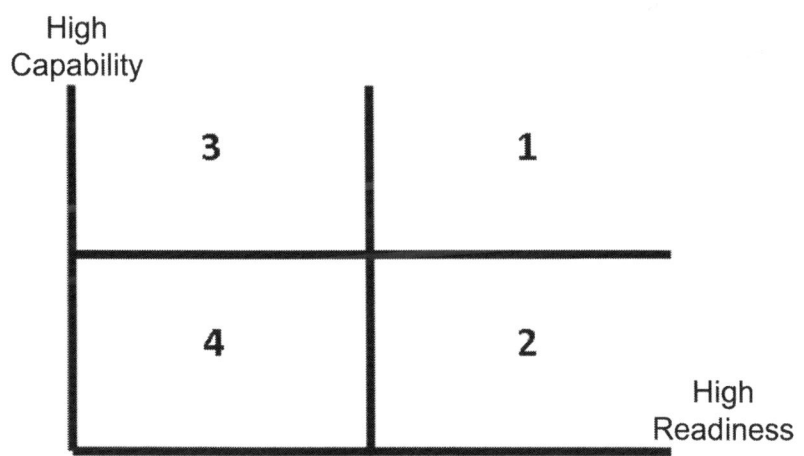

Figure. 8 Readiness and Capability analysis

Developing a toolkit for change and sharing it with your team helps change to be seen as a joint endeavour and responsibility, not just the province of the leader. You would not expect to use the tools we have looked at for all changes but, for the changes that will have the biggest impact on children's learning, the ones which we need to get right, they are invaluable.

Appreciative Inquiry

Sometimes a Middle Leader might be joining a school or team where, for whatever reason, morale is very low. Perhaps the school has had a poor Ofsted, a succession of leaders in a short space of time or some other problem which has impacted on the team. An approach to change known as Appreciative Inquiry can sometimes be very helpful in these circumstances. This was developed by the Canadian academics, David Cooperrider and Suresh Srivasta (1987). This method of planning change has a number of advantages for low morale in that it:

- is future orientated rather than backward looking
- starts with a success rather than a problem
- treats organisations as organic, a set of relationships

Briefly the process consists of four stages: *Discovery, Dream, Design* and *Deliver.*

In the Discovery phase those involved in the change, which could be the whole staff or a particular team, gather information about the things they do best and why. This is not a superficial exercise; they must really examine in great detail why this aspect of their work has been successful. They may look at the work in detail, interview children, look at planning etc. In the Dream stage, they concentrate on what they want to improve and envision the ideal future in terms of the issue they are focussing on.

Again, this needs to be done in detail. What would the work look like if we did succeed? How would our work in the classroom be different? How would the work we are assessing look different? etc. They then Design a path to achieve the Dream which often involves projects, actions or experiments. Finally, in the Deliver stage, programmes for implementation are designed. More information on Appreciative Inquiry approaches is readily available on the internet. It has the disadvantage that the process of planning the change can take longer but is particularly effective where there may be a sense of failure in a team or where the change is particularly sensitive. Appreciative Inquiry ensures that because the whole team is involved in the process of change you get high levels of commitment to the change.

Transformational or Transactional Leadership

The tools and processes we have looked at so far are useful for managing any change within a team. There are, however, many different theories as to the leadership style most appropriate for particular changes, especially cultural changes. James MacGregor Burns (1978) was an historian and political scientist and first introduced the concepts of Transformational and Transactional Leadership. He defined Transformational and Transactional leaders as follows:

Transactional Leaders work in existing cultures. They create clear structures, clarify roles, establish goals, monitor and provide positive and negative rewards. It can be argued that this is the most common approach to leadership in most schools. Sometimes, Burns argues, this approach is not effective. Where the problems in an organisation can only be addressed by a change in culture, a Transformational Leadership approach is more effective. Covey (Covey, S. R., Principle-centred leadership. New York : Fireside 1990) states that:

The goal of Transformational Leadership is to 'transform' people and organisations in a literal sense – to change them in mind and heart; enlarge vision, insight, and understanding; clarify purposes; make behaviour congruent with beliefs, principles, or values; and bring about changes that are permanent, self-perpetuating, and momentum building.

To achieve this change in hearts and minds and transform the vision for your team requires an approach to leadership built on four components:
- Charisma or idealised influence—getting your team to identify with your beliefs
- Inspirational motivation—modelling high values and conveying an inspiring vision
- Intellectual stimulation—encouraging the team to look at issues from a new perspective
- Individualised consideration—coaching, support and encouragement for individuals

In practical terms a transformational approach could be more effective in a situation where you take over a team with a history of poor performance, where tweaking is unlikely to achieve the level of change needed. Some of the work of Headteachers and other school leaders in Inner City Academies could be characterised as transformational. Transformational leaders operate at the higher levels of the Maslow (1943) hierarchy and thus need to establish and maintain high levels of authenticity.

The language of transformational leaders is very different from transactional leaders. Often transactional leaders will use phrases such as *must do...*, *have to...*, *need to...* etc.

Transformational leaders would be using language such as *we have the opportunity to..., only the best will be good enough for...* etc.

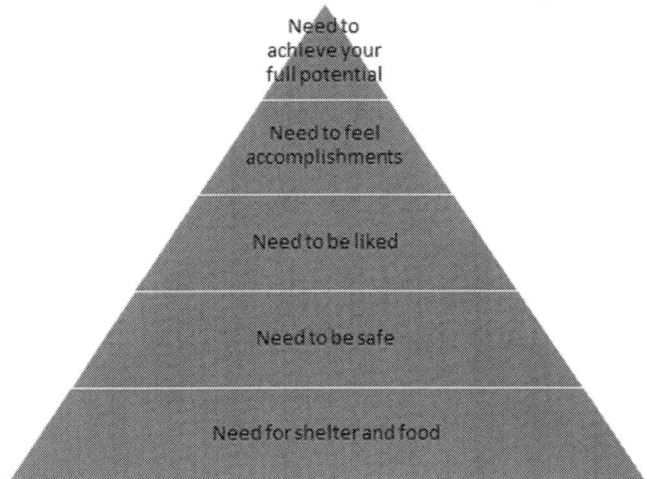

Figure 9. Maslow's hierarchy of need

Transformational language comes easily to some leaders but others need to develop the ability to talk to staff in this way. Reminding staff how important what they do is, and the high responsibilities they have in terms of preparing future generations, can be much more motivating than using the threat of Ofsted as a reason for introducing change.

Key Points
- Manage change using processes understood by all the team in order to develop trust and ownership of change.
- Important changes are worth planning and managing carefully.

Further reading;
Kotter J, (1996) *Leading Change* Harvard Business School Press. ISBN 0875847471

Johnson S, (1998) *Who moved my cheese?* Publisher: Vermilion. ISBN 0091816971

CHAPTER THREE
Developing Others and Yourself
• • •

'Leaders become great not because of their power but their ability to empower others'
John Maxwell

According to a 2003 report on the role of Middle Leadership in schools, produced by the National College of School Leadership, "Subject Leaders' authority comes not from their position but their competence as teachers and their subject knowledge". Thus, maintaining and improving your teaching skills as a Middle Leader is a task of the utmost importance. We have already talked of the need to continually reflect and learn about leadership, but your subject specialism or curriculum area should also be a priority for your learning. Keeping up to date and well networked with colleagues carrying out similar roles in other schools is one way of helping to achieve this and is a really important part of the Middle Leader's role. Knowledge gained in this way needs to be cascaded to your team as part of your regular meetings. These meetings will also provide opportunities for sharing what they have learned. Making professional development a key part of what happens when you meet with the team is a very effective way of growing your capacity to improve.

There are many ways to develop your skills as a leader, but as we have seen, none are more effective than mentoring and coaching.

In education we are often given a mentor when we change or take on a role. Mentors are useful in that they can problem solve for us in new, unfamiliar circumstances. However, mentoring is a deficit model, the paradigm being that the mentor knows more than the mentee and, although initially it helps to build confidence, if mentoring goes on for too long, it can in fact help develop learned helplessness and lack of confidence. At some stage the support needs to move into coaching which is not a deficit model. All leaders can benefit from coaching and you should ensure that as a Middle Leader you have a coach. There will be many benefits that flow from this, one of which is that you will become more able and better equipped to coach your team.

As a Middle Leader you may have limited control over the whole school staff development programme, although it is good to be an advocate of the opportunity for your team to train together on inset days. You will have more control over what happens when the team meets together and whenever this happens some time should be spent on professional development. This could take many forms, but the following are useful and effective activities in terms of building your team into a professional learning community:

- Good practice hot seats- information on my best recent lesson- learning conversation about why this worked.
- Discussion of previously distributed 'think piece'. What are the implications, if any, for our practice?
- Cascading learning from courses, network visits.
- Sharing results of action research.
- Looking in depth at a small area of planning and relate it to children's learning.
- Looking at videos of teaching and having a learning conversation about what is seen.
- Discussing what has been learnt from peer observation.

- Collaborative planning.
- Lesson Study.

The above list is not an exhaustive, but these type of activities can be used to help establish learning as the focus of your meetings. Inevitably everyday issues and problems will also be discussed at meetings but improving learning should always be at the heart of what takes place.

The work of Joyce and Showers has demonstrated that sending people on courses is far less likely to lead to a change in practice than coaching. The difference can be large, from a 5% chance of changing practice when going on a course to over 90% chance of a change in practice when working with a coach. The potential for coaching your team thus provides your best opportunity as a leader to build the capacity for improvement. This does not necessarily mean timetabling coaching sessions, although these can be extremely effective, but in adopting a coaching approach to everyday interactions with your team. This is typified by asking powerful questions which lead to new insights and adopting an inquiry-based approach to problems rather than jumping to solutions. This more reflective approach in your relationships with your team will model good leadership behaviours for them and make them more reflective practitioners. Making time for professional development within the team is not easy and activities such as peer observation can be expensive and cause some disruption.

The use of video in the classroom

The increasing use of video has provided new opportunities for professional development.

If we consider the model of professional development shown in Figure 10, we can use video to facilitate learning in all of the important areas shown. The equipment used for videoing can vary enormously in terms of price but in fact need not be expensive. A simple wide angled lensed video camera and tripod will generate a tremendous amount of useful information. Similarly, an Ipad on a stand can be used effectively. Some staff, however, can be very anxious about filming themselves. If you are going to use video with your team it is important to establish a protocol to address these anxieties. Typically, the protocol might include an acknowledgement that videoing is an activity for volunteers. You can, however, encourage its use by filming yourself, in order to model how it can be used to improve teaching and learning. Each video recording should also be the property of the teacher being filmed so that they can choose whether to share it or not.

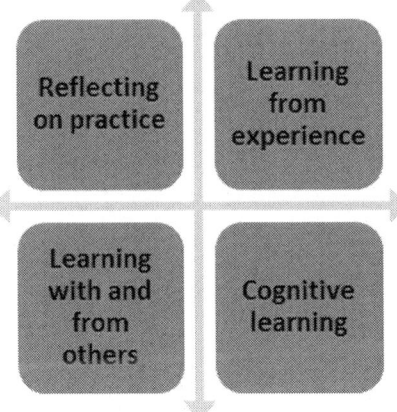

Figure 10. A model for Professional Development

The reason video is so useful is it gives a truer picture of the learning that takes place in our classrooms. When somebody comes in to observe us, inevitably they change the dynamic of the lesson they observe. We can also use video to record the responses of children and dig more deeply into their learning. As long as such recordings are only watched by staff at the school there

would be no need to get parental consent for this activity, and it opens up a whole new way of monitoring and improving learning. Videos can also be a very effective starting point for a coaching conversation using, for example, questions such as:
- Which child do we think learnt most and why?
- How did you choose who to ask that question?
- What activity do you think was the most successful and why?

The whole team could take part in such coaching discussions.

A recent report on coaching by the Centre for British Teachers (CFBT) found the use of video to be one of the most effective focusses for coaching, so although you might meet with some initial resistance, it is worth trying to develop its use as a tool. In my experience teachers find it incredibly useful and soon become advocates once they have tried it.

Evidence based improvement

Whenever we engage in professional learning it is important that the approaches we use are rigorous and valid, especially for the context within which we are working. When we carry out action research in our own schools and with our own children, we know that it is valid and generates what is sometimes called 'sticky knowledge'. This means the findings are likely to prove useful to other colleagues in the school. Naturally, however, we will want to look at what others have learnt, sometimes through academic texts, courses or network visits. When trying new approaches, sourced in this way, it is always a good idea to check that they work in your own context. Each team is different and what works for some will not work for others. Your job as team leader is to ensure that an evidence-based approach to improvements in learning is always followed by the team.

Collaborative lesson planning

Joyce and Showers (1996) in their book 'The evolution of coaching' argue that the most successful context in which to coach is when staff are co-planning work. Their belief is that in this situation staff are more comfortable providing the sort of challenge that is most useful for learning through coaching. 'Research lessons,' an NCTL initiative, and 'Lesson Study' a similar initiative developed within the National Strategies, provide a framework for this type of joint planning. (The internet has a lot of information on Research Lessons and Lesson Study, including examples of their use). In both models, staff work together to plan an input that will be delivered in a way that is different from the approach the teacher would usually have taken or has taken in the past. An example might be a topic that they have never been entirely happy teaching.

The teacher is supported in this planning by one or two colleagues depending on which of the models is used. The reason for involving other colleagues is to reduce the risk averseness in the planning process, so that the teacher sees this as a joint learning activity not a pass/ fail activity which puts them at risk. When planning, they focus on a small number of learners e.g. three, and the detailed planning for the new approach is focussed around these three learners. (Planning templates are available in 'Lesson Study': a handbook published by Lesson Study UK) The reason for this is that the observations, carried out by the teacher and at least one colleague, can be focussed on these children. Video could also be used. The learners can also be interviewed afterwards about their experiences in the lesson. This approach ensures a rich, focussed discussion about the learning that took place rather than a more generalised discussion that can occur when talking about class reaction rather than that of individual learners. Sometimes it might be useful to choose the learners for a specific reason from the teaching group. If, for example, the reason the teacher would like to change the way the lesson is delivered is because they feel in the past it has not stretched the high attainers, then they might choose to use three high attaining learners to focus on. Equally, it could be three low attainers if they were concerned about their learning using their current approach. If there is no particular focus, then the three learners could be chosen to represent the full attainment range. At the end, when the new approach has been tried, and all the evidence gathered is discussed, the teacher decides on any permanent changes to the way this work is taught in the future and any general implications for their teaching.

Pupil Voice

Another key aspect to improving learning is how you engage with the learners in order to get their feedback about the learning experiences. Some aspects of this engagement have come to be known as Pupil Voice. Pupil Voice has, I believe, a huge potential to improve learning, if used effectively.

Pupil Voice, in the form of school councils etc., has existed for some time and has often been involved in very worthy, but perhaps not key issues within the school. There have, however, been some far more exciting examples of involving learners in issues that affect them, and in particular their learning. Some examples of these approaches are:

- Having an improvement team made up of learners, focusing on your area of responsibility.
- Lesson observations carried out by learners. (If staff find this threatening, starting with an appreciative inquiry approach to feedback, discussed below, is a good way to begin.)
- Consultation evenings between parent, teacher and the learner, which are chaired by the learner.

- A school environmental team formed by learners, making recommendations, in order that the school can operate in a more sustainable way.

The schools that use Pupil Voice in this way are not playing lip service to the concept but involving learners in important issues, giving them real influence in improving the school. Getting feedback from learners is essential if schools are serious about improving learning and indeed Hattie (2008) in his book 'Visible learning' argues that feedback from learners is the most important type of feedback. As a Middle Leader you will have the opportunity of making this a priority for your team and modelling getting feedback from children for all your staff.

Getting feedback using Appreciative Inquiry

We have already seen that an Appreciative Inquiry approach can be used in the management of change. Appreciative Inquiry also provides a method of getting feedback which is especially appropriate in areas where there are sensitivities. Feedback is the gap between intention and perception and any method that tests that gap can provide useful feedback. You could use a 360 degree feedback approach to do this, but sometimes staff can find this threatening and it does not always successfully lead to improvement. Appreciative Inquiry seeks feedback by asking questions for which there are only positive answers. One advantage to this method is that people will tell you the truth because they do not feel the feedback damages people in the way some other methods can do. Nonetheless, in-spite of the technique not being seen as threatening, it can still open the gap between intention and perception. Some examples of Appreciative Inquiry feedback questions are shown below.

For pupils:
- What makes learning fun for you?
- What is the best thing about this class?
- Who is the best person to speak to if you have a problem?
- What is the best thing I can do to help your learning?
- What activity helped you learn best this week?
- What did you enjoy most this week?
- When you have a problem with your learning what is the best thing I can do to help?
- What is the most important thing you have learnt about how you learn?
- What activities in the classroom do you enjoy most?
- What makes you want to work hard?

Feedback for you from your team!
- When am I most positive?
- When am I most enthusiastic?
- What do I role model?
- What is my best quality as a leader?
- What values do I articulate?
- What is my best quality as a team member?
- What is the most important thing I do in the school?
- What do I do to build good relationships with and between staff?
- When am I most helpful in supporting you in doing your job?
- What is the most effective thing I do to support you when you have difficulties?
- When you want support, what behaviours do I exhibit that are most supportive?
- What has been the best change I have introduced?

Whenever we get feedback we were not expecting, we have a gap between our intentions and other people's perceptions. We can reflect on this and may sometimes decide to change a behaviour in order to change the perception. At other times we might to decide to live with the gap, but at least we are aware of it. Whatever we think about other peoples' perceptions, that is their reality and we have to accept it as such. As a teacher when you look at the questions above, you can immediately see how useful it would be to have your pupils' views on their learning.

Delegation.

You may have been helped on your journey to Middle Leadership by working for a leader who gave you opportunities for learning about leadership by delegating tasks to you. As a Middle Leader you have the opportunity to do the same for members of your team. Some Middle Leaders shy away from this because, from experience, they find staff continually keep checking with them to ensure they are doing the right thing and it seems almost quicker to do the job yourself. This is often symptomatic of not making it clear to staff the level of authority they have, in order to carry out the task you have given them. Often leaders are much better at delegating tasks than delegating the authority to do them! In order to effectively empower a member of staff to carry out a task, the first step is to brief them thoroughly about the area of responsibility you are giving them and the things you want them to take into consideration etc when carrying out the responsibility. Taking the time to be as explicit as possible about this saves time later. You also need to be explicit with them, and with any other staff involved, about the authority you are giving them in order to carry out the task. Finally, you need to ensure that you build in some time to hold them to account for what they do. If any of these elements are missing, empowerment is only partial and the need for continual checking is sometimes an indicator of this. Delegation always involves an element of letting go and overcoming the temptation to micromanage, which is at the root of many time management issues. It is also wise to avoid delegating the things you don't like doing as this quickly becomes recognised as 'dumping'. To whom and what to delegate is a key part of delegation.

Think of empowerment as a tripod—if one leg is missing it doesn't work!

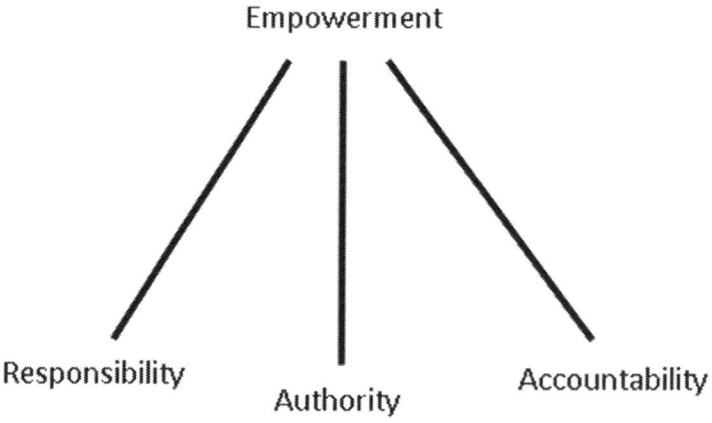

Fig. 11 Empowerment diagram

We tend to be good in schools at giving people responsibility but without the authority to carry things out and this leads to frustration for the person we have delegated the task to. If we give authority but without checking and giving feedback through accountability systems, we run the risk of the person going off in a direction we are not happy with. Good delegation is a fine balance between these things but is essential not only because of its impact on time management but on the leadership development of staff. Jim Collins (2001) gives some good advice on delegation when he says get your best people to work on your greatest opportunities not your biggest problems.

Key Points
- Make professional learning a top priority.
- Get a coach and coach others.
- Use feedback effectively.

Further reading:
Rath T, (2009) *Strength Based Leadership* Gallup Press ISBN-10: 1595620257

Chapter Four
Securing Accountability
• • •

'Accountability is essential to personal growth, as well as team growth. How can you improve if you're never wrong? If you don't admit a mistake and take responsibility for it, you're bound to make the same one again.'
Pat Summitt

The research on Middle Leadership reveals that holding members of their team accountable is the aspect of the role new leaders find most worrying, and the one they are most reluctant to take on. This is often due to anxiety about having what they imagine are difficult conversations with people they work closely with. Indeed, at times, they may need to do so. However, ducking these occasional difficult conversations, which your team will expect you to take on, will result in you losing credibility as a leader. Accountability, in any team or organisation, is a key part of its success since it facilitates improvement, alignment of effort and personal growth of team members. All too often, however, accountability is associated with blame, resentment and unfairness. As a Middle Leader you cannot change accountability systems that exist in your school, but you can implement them in a fair and honest way. If you are involved in the Performance Management of your team it is wise to model and interpret accountability as answerability. Not only is this fair because we are all answerable for what we do, but it helps us understand what the process involves. In order to get answers, we must ask questions, and this is at the heart of the accountability process. If, as a leader in progress meetings with staff, I find myself making all the suggestions for improvement, then I will be responsible and accountable for what happens as a result, not them. Of course, I can offer advice, especially for less experienced staff, but most of the suggestions for improvement should come from them. I can again facilitate this process by asking good questions to promote new thinking and using evidence to ensure impact and rigour.

As a Middle Leader there are many levels of personal accountability. Although, nowadays Ofsted looms large when we think of accountability, your real accountability will be to the children who are learning in the area you are responsible for. Using the threat of Ofsted as a way of trying to increase the accountability of your team is very risky since not many staff are motivated by this. Reminding them of the important part they play in the life chances of the children they teach will work much better!

Ofsted and Middle Leaders

The quality of Middle Leadership is a particular focus for Ofsted and as a Middle Leader you may well be interviewed as part of a school inspection.

The following is some advice about what you need to know, and to prepare for an Ofsted inspection, developed by the National Association of Headteachers.

1. What are the strengths in your subject/area of responsibility? How do you know this?
   Tips: Be prepared to identify 2-3 key strengths, don't try to cover too many. Make sure they genuinely are strengths and that you have the evidence to back up your claims e.g. data or evidence from your monitoring activities.
2. What are the key areas for development/weaknesses to address?

Tips: Don't try to hide any obvious areas for development—it is better to be honest and explain what you are doing to address these. Again, pick the top priorities here rather than embark on a long list.

3. What have been your key priorities for improvement in recent years and what impact have these actions had on pupil outcomes?
Tips: Consider what you have already done to improve standards and be prepared to articulate the strategy as well as the positive impact it had e.g. "I introduced X, and as a result attainment went up by Y%".

4. How well do pupils achieve in your subject/area of responsibility?
Tips: If there is national data available, make sure you use this i.e. be prepared to talk about how attainment and progress of pupils in your subject/area compare to the national picture. Make sure you point to both current data of pupils still in the school as well as historic data.

5. Are there any discrepancies in achievement between different groups of pupils?
Tips: It is important to be aware of any particular issues there might be for specific groups of pupils. Do certain groups appear to achieve better or worse than their peers? A focus on SEND, those eligible for pupil premium, higher attaining pupils, gender and ethnicity are all important to consider.

6. What work are you doing to close any achievement gaps, especially for those eligible for pupil premium funding?
Tips: You will be expected to be aware of any gaps that might exist. Closing the gap between disadvantaged pupils and their peers remains a major national priority so be prepared to talk about your work in this area.

7. How do you assess learning and pupil progress in your area of responsibility?
   Tips: Since the end of national curriculum levels there is a renewed emphasis on leaders being able to articulate how learning is assessed and, critically, how any information is used to help improve the progress pupils make. Remember, there is no one correct way to do this—you just need to be able to articulate how your school does this in a clear and coherent manner. What you do with the data is more important that how you collect it so try to focus on this.
8. How do you monitor standards in your subject/area of responsibility?
   Tips: Remember that monitoring takes a variety of forms e.g. pupil conferencing, lesson observations, book sampling, data analysis etc. How do you use this information to draw conclusions and, critically, what do you do as a result?
9. What is the quality of teaching like in your subject/area of responsibility?
   Tips: Be prepared to talk about how well your subject is taught. Where is it taught well/less well? Are there particular strengths or weaknesses in terms of teaching? Be prepared to be quite specific here e.g. "number and place value is taught well, but we are working on how we teach problem solving effectively." You may need to be specific in terms of the quality of teaching across the school e.g. "Teaching is strong in the upper school, but not yet as strong in the lower school."
10. How involved are you in improving the practice of colleagues in your school?
    Tips: Have you been involved in mentoring new teach-

ers/coaching more experienced ones? If so, consider how you have helped improved their practice? What would you do if you identify an issue in terms of quality of teaching?

11. Is there a CPD plan for your area of responsibility?
Tips: Be prepared to talk through how you co-ordinate, plan or lead training for colleagues in your area of responsibility. Is there a plan in place and does this link to your wider improvement plan?

12. How do the senior leaders in the school support you in your role? Do you receive CPD as a middle leader?
Tips: Consider how you work with senior leaders. Do you meet regularly? This is not the time to launch into a list of complaints about lack of support from senior leaders—probably better to have these conversations separately!

Checking Conversations.

Checking conversations were mentioned as part of the spectrum of conversations in Chapter 1. These are very important conversations for a leader to have because they are concerned with quality assurance. The other important reason for having checking conversations is that if you have these regularly as a leader you can avoid many of the difficult conversations that might otherwise result. Thus, if I introduce a change of policy for the team I need to check that it has been implemented. This can be done formally or informally. Suppose, for example I have introduced a new assessment system as a result of some the processes mentioned in Chapter 2. Subsequently, I could say to a member of staff at the end of the day perhaps 'How are you finding the new assessment system?' If the response is 'I haven't tried it yet', or 'I have been too busy to try it', then I can re-iterate that we have agreed as a team this needs doing and ask them to start implementation without delay. This type of checking is especially important when I know I have a member of staff who is likely not to have implemented the change. Checking is also important in terms of whole school policies, not just initiatives within your subject area. Consistency of implementation is key to the success of all school policies and you will need to make sure that your team are contributing to this.

Use of data

The use and interpretation of data has become a key aspect of leadership and plays an important part in Performance Management. As a leader it is your responsibility to make sure that you understand the validity and accuracy of the data you are dealing with. In recent times, almost all teachers have gained a greater awareness of the use of data, but it is still important to remember that data can only raise an issue to be addressed, it is not an end in itself. Thus, just saying the percentage reaching national standard in reading is not good enough and will cause all sorts of problems should we have an Ofsted, will not in itself lead to a solution. As a leader I need to work with the staff to create real clarity about what they need to do differently in order to improve things and deliver better results. Establishing this clarity will also increase their accountability for delivering the improvement. While the conversation focuses on the outcome and is unclear about the change needed, there will be much less accountability. Once you have mastered the data it is important to ensure that your team has a good grasp of the what the data is telling you. One important aspect of data collection that tends to be ignored is that it also tells you where you are doing well, as well as indicating areas where you might look for improvement. Understanding why you are doing well and building on that strength is an important process for your team.

Dealing with blocking

Most staff are very happy to work with leaders to ensure that they get the best from Performance Management but just occasionally a leader will come across a member of staff who tries to block them. Blocking is defined as a failure to take responsibility.

Sometimes when trying to hold a member of staff to account you may meet some blocking. This will often, but not exclusively, take the form of excuses and blaming others; 'The problem is the children in this class...the lack of time or the resources I have... the teaching assistant I have.' Fortunately blocking does not occur very often but it important to understand how to deal with blocking. Typical blocking techniques include:
- Failure to take responsibility
- Changing the subject
- Compliance
- Flooding with detail

Fortunately, there are well known techniques for dealing with blocking. The most effective way to deal with blocking assertively is to name the blocking technique the person is using and then use silence to make the person blocking respond. In responding they take ownership of the behaviour and you can move forward. An example might be a teacher who, when asked about the lack of progress of some of the learners in his/her class, continually talks about behaviour issues or other problems rather than what they might do to address the progress issue. If this persists beyond what might be reasonable under the circumstances, given that this might not be an easy class, but in order to give them ownership of the issue you could say:

> You are not saying, are you, that there is nothing you could do differently to address the problem you have regarding the progress of these learners?

You would then have to remain silent until they respond. If you drive into the silence you take the responsibility away from them and they don't take ownership of the issue. If you avoid this and remain silent, typically after a rather awkward period they may say something like 'well I suppose I could do something different...' they then take ownership of the issue and we can move forward. As Susan Scott says in her book 'Fierce Conversations' (2002) 'let silence do the heavy lifting'. The same approach could be used for the other methods of blocking such as continually changing the subject, compliance and flooding with detail. In these cases, you might say:

> You keep changing the subject. I can't tell what you think is at the core of the problem you have with the progress of learners in your class.

> You seem to agree with almost any strategy suggested. I can't tell what you think is the key to the problem you have with progress of learners in your class.

> You keep flooding me with detail. I can't tell what you think is at the core of the problem you have with progress of the learners in your class.

More often than not, the person will move towards you, sometimes reluctantly, but you will immediately follow this up by supporting them in moving forward.

e.g. In response to 'Well I suppose there may be something I could do differently'

I might say 'What area of your practice do you think it would be useful to focus on then?' We can then begin to explore their suggestions for what they might do differently and the potential impact this would have.

This unblocking technique is remarkably successful but just occasionally somebody may come back with 'I have tried everything' or 'I can't think of anything to do'. Again, the leader has to respond with a question or statement that will make them take responsibility e.g. 'Do you think anybody could have tried everything?', 'Where could you access some new thinking'.

Unblocking is a win-win for leaders in that it makes people accountable who are avoiding accountability, but at the same time moves them from a situation where they feel helpless to one where they are more empowered. Trying to move around a block does not work. If I get so frustrated that I end up making suggestions as to what they should do differently, without removing the block, not only do I become accountable, but they have an interest, perhaps unconsciously, in not making the suggestion work. This would support their belief that there is nothing to be done.

The ability to have difficult conversations without upsetting the person you are dealing with any more than you need to, is a real leadership skill. You should be trying to achieve 'acceptance' after a difficult conversation. I would define this as the person still not liking what has happened during the conversation but understanding the reasons you had to have it. Here are some general tips to help with difficult conversations.

1. State clearly what the problem is you are addressing and avoid ambiguity.
2. Avoid opinion and stick to evidence. Using opinion can too easily lead to a difference of opinion and conflict. There will now be a winner and a loser, and the process will be even more emotional. Using evidence helps reduce the chance of this.
3. *Listen* to what the person has to say.
4. When giving somebody a message they don't want to hear be clear about any decisions you are taking, the evidence on

which the decision is based, and tell them what the downside is for them. If you don't, they will tell you and you will have a more negative meeting. By doing this it will also show that you have thought about this from their perspective and thus is more likely to lead to acceptance.

Dealing with underperformance.

Dealing with the underperformance of team members is probably the most difficult job that Middle Leaders can face. Sometimes this underperformance is associated with blocking which we have dealt with above. Ensuring that the team member you are working with feels accountable is essential if you are going to be able to support them in improving. This support may take the form of mentoring and coaching or any of the other developmental activities we have already mentioned. Usually with this kind of targeted support, where clear measurable targets are set for people, you will be able to get improvement in performance. However, if their best is just not good enough you must ensure that official procedures are invoked, difficult though this might be. The children rely on you as a leader to do this, as will the other members of the team. The difference between a high performing teacher and low performing teacher can be enormous in terms of children's learning and cannot be ignored. The Sutton Trust in its report 'Improving the impact of teachers on pupil achievement in the UK—interim findings.' September 2011 found:

'The difference between a very effective teacher and a poorly performing teacher is large. For example, during one year with a very effective Maths teacher, pupils gain 40% more in their learning than they would with a poorly performing Maths teacher'.

Closing that gap between the best performing team members and the least good ones, is a key task for you as a Middle Leader.

Building on strengths

When it comes to the personal development aspects of Performance Management it is tempting to focus almost exclusively on performance gaps. However, there is a growing body of evidence that it is more profitable to focus on further developing strengths. The paper on Strength Based development produced by 'Engaging Minds' (https://engagingminds.co.uk/sbr/wp-content/uploads/2014/11/Strengths-based-development-QA-Engaging-Minds.pdf) has some good evidence to support this approach. If you were to choose one strength and one gap as personal development targets in Performance Management, this might help staff to be more positive about the process and not always see it as a deficit model.

Another kind of difficult conversation I am often asked about is how, as a Middle Leader, do I disagree with the Headteacher? This can be a delicate situation, but criticising is always best done with a good question rather than seeking a confrontation by stating opinions you know the other person will disagree with. As we have seen, a good question can open up new perspectives and opportunities. Some of the questions previously listed could be used in this situation. One very effective method of avoiding conflict is to ask somebody 'What are you seeing with regard to this issue that I am not seeing?' and then listening very carefully to what they say. Repeating back will show them you have listened, and they will now give you permission to tell them what you are seeing that they may not be. Often this will lead to a negotiation and compromise. In this way we can deal with the problem without turning it into a conflict. Although there are no professional standards for Middle Leaders in England, the General Teaching Council for Scotland have done some very useful work in defining the role of Middle Leaders. This is available in their 2012 publication 'The Standards for Leadership and Management: supporting leadership and management development' available from their web-site at http://www.gtcs.org.uk.

Reflective practitioners

We have known for some time that the most effective teachers are reflective practitioners. The same is true for leaders. Those leaders who learn from experience, and are able to use that learning to improve, are far more effective. Reflecting on situations where things go particularly badly or particularly well is especially important. These are critical incidents and can have a profound effect on your learning. There are many frameworks to help you structure your reflections but one of the simplest and most useful was developed by Gibbs (1988). Gibb's reflective cycle can be really useful in making you think through all the phases of an experience or activity and is shown below in Figure 12. It is important to ensure that you go through each stage and are as honest with yourself as you can be.

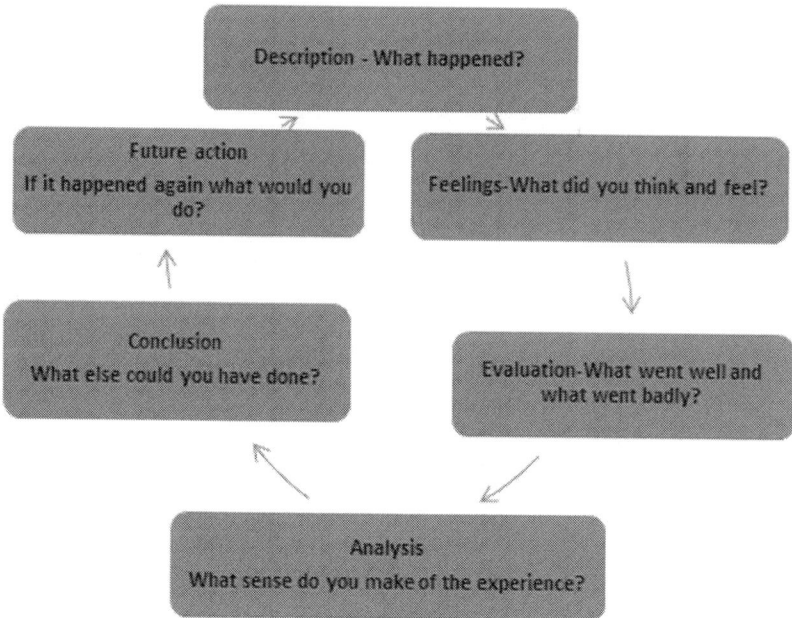

Figure 12. Gibbs reflective cycle

Key Points

- When done well, Performance Management is motivating and leads to improvement.
- Don't duck difficult conversations, just get better at them!

Further reading:

Scott S, (2002) *Fierce Conversations.* Publisher Judy Piatkuss. ISBN 0670031240

Brundrett M, Rhodes C, (2010) *Leadership for Quality and Accountability in Education.* Routledge ISBN 978-0-415-37874-1

CHAPTER FIVE

Developing Pedagogy and Becoming a Leader of Learning
• • •

> *'I never learn anything talking. I only learn things when I ask questions.'*
> Lou Holtz

Since learning is the core purpose for the work of your team, a large part of the judgement about how successful your leadership is will be measured by the effect you have on improving learning within your area of responsibility. How leaders impact on learning has come to be known as 'Learning-Centred Leadership'. In recent years there has been a sharp focus on this area of leadership and some of the best insights have come from Professor Geoff Southworth at the National College of Teaching and Leadership. (Middle Leadership in primary schools project 2006).

He believes that learning-centred leaders can have the biggest impact on what happens in the classroom through modelling, dialogue and monitoring (through good accountability structures). We have touched on the importance of these before but one further insight he provides into modelling is that learning-centred leaders manage their modelling in order to support any changes they are trying to put in place. He calls this 'managing the indirect effects of leadership.' Thus, if one of our key priorities as a school is improving writing then you can make this a focus of some of your leadership behaviours for the year; examples might be making this a focus when carrying out formal observations, having formal and informal dialogue with staff and learners and during formal meetings. This will be a powerful tool to support the change because we know that modelling by the leader can be very influential. Professor John West Burnham has also written on learning-centred leadership (think piece for NCSL Leading Learning and Teaching – Learning-Centred Leadership) and has added coaching to the things the leader can do to impact on learning in the classroom. I believe this is an important addition to how we think of learning-centred leadership and it is certainly important for Middle Leaders to be able to coach members of their team. The focus of this coaching should always be improving learning in the classroom.

A dialogue about learning

Learning is a complex process and one we are still working to fully understand. Because of this there is often no agreed language of learning which teachers, students and parents can share, unless leaders help create one. The question to ask yourself is: when I use the word learning what are my team and other stakeholders hearing? In creating a shared, coherent view of what learning is amongst stakeholders, you open up a huge potential for raising standards. This shared language, often based on a model of learning, may consist of just thirty or forty key words that are shared between teachers, learners and parents.

Developing a shared language and understanding of learning, offers a number of really important advantages, some of which are listed below:
- Children would have a greater understanding of what learning involved and be empowered to be independent learners.
- Opportunities for developing meta-cognition would be greatly increased.

- Teachers would be more confident that they were extending children's learning.
- Professional learning would be more focussed and effective.
- Learning objectives would be more fully understood by both teachers and learners.
- Feedback would be more fully understood by children and therefore more useful.
- Parents could support learning more effectively.
- Behaviour for learning becomes a concept that children understand.

Two examples are shown below. (Fig. 13 & Fig. 14)

Figure 13. Primary Learning model and shared language developed with a Primary School

Once the learning vocabulary has been agreed, teachers need to try to use these words in Learning Objectives and feedback, and check with children that they have a clear understanding of the learning words and processes associated with them.

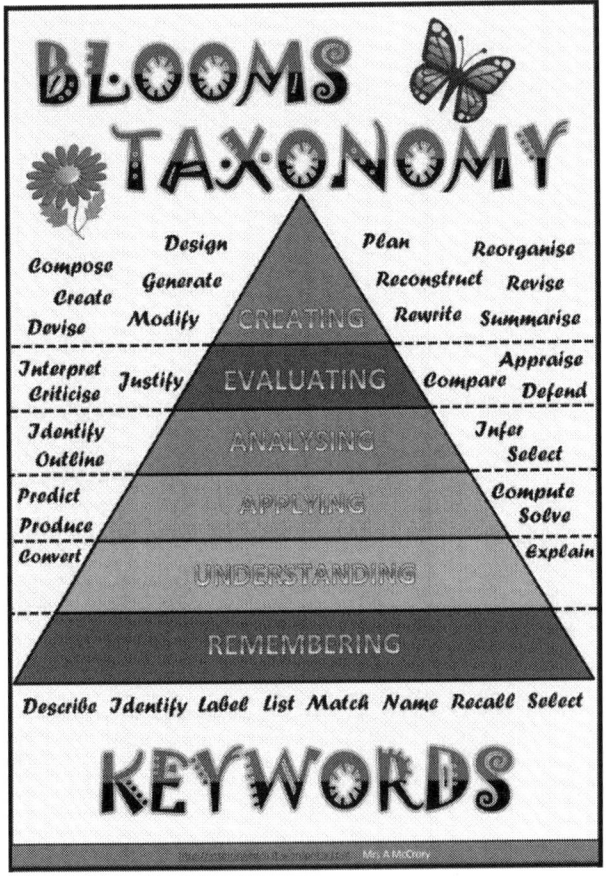

Figure 14. Secondary Learning model and shared language

By choosing words that regularly occur in examinations in your subject area, this helps avoid the problem of children not understanding clearly what they are being asked to do in an examination. It is also a very effective way of developing more independent learners; when learners themselves actually have a clearer understanding of learning, they are better equipped to manage their own learning. Similarly, parents are able to support their children's learning more effectively, if they have a greater understanding of the learning process. If your team agrees a model of learning to focus on, it can be displayed in all classrooms and, in time, will become well understood and internalised by both staff and children.

Models of Learning

Although there are no definitive models of learning, looking at the research can help you begin this process of building a shared understanding and language around learning.

A good starting place is Bloom's taxonomy of learning. The two models shown in Figures 13 and 14 are based on Bloom's taxonomy. Bloom's taxonomy was developed by Benjamin Bloom in 1956. His original work is summarised in Figure 15 and was mainly used to develop more effective questioning. In 2001 a revised taxonomy, expressed as verbs, was developed by Anderson and Krathwohl (2001). Biggs and Collis (1982) also built on the work of Bloom and developed Solo taxonomy which is widely used in New Zealand. I have worked with schools which begin using models such as Bloom's taxonomy or Solo taxonomy and go on to develop their own model, based on a structure and vocabulary they are happy with and feel is appropriate for their students. This is then displayed in every classroom and forms the basis of the dialogue about learning. Having some sort of agreement about the learning process can also help staff feel far more confident that they are supporting learners in their classroom.

There are some wonderful resources available on the internet, such as lists of Bloom's and Solo questions and verbs, to support this process. The average teacher asks over 400 questions a day, very few of which require higher level thinking. In my experience, the use of Bloom's will transform this and improve learning. The illustrations below give a visual impression of the Bloom's and Solo taxonomies. (Figs. 15 and 16)

Bloom's original Taxonomy 1956

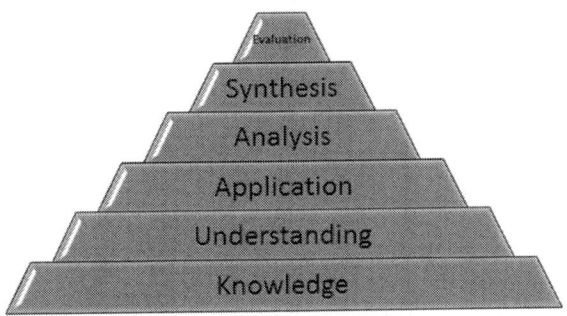

Bloom's Revised Taxonomy 2001

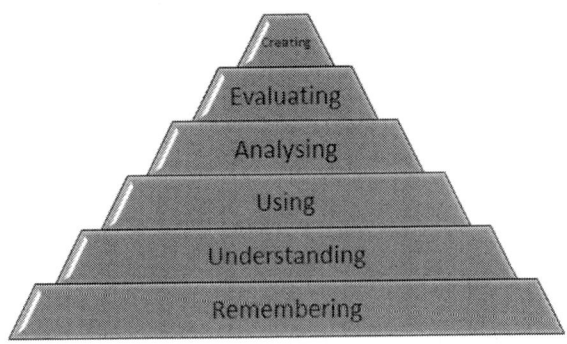

Figure 15. Bloom's original and revised taxonomies

The Middle Leader's Toolkit

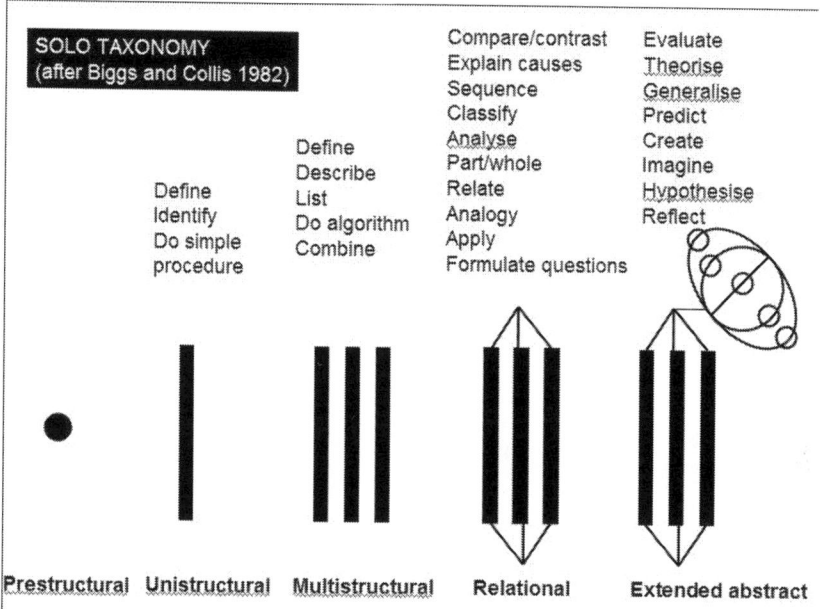

Figure 16. Solo taxonomy

Both Bloom's and Solo taxonomies promote higher level thinking. They also demonstrate that all children can think at higher levels if the context of the learning is appropriate. For example, a five year old child being read a story can be asked how they think it will end and why they think this (synthesis) or which character they like best and why (evaluation). This is important in helping to raise expectations about what children can do and showing all children can achieve higher level thinking. Important to note: the earlier they start it the better they get at it. Higher level thinking in a particular curriculum area, will also promote better retention and transference of knowledge, and will support children in achieving higher standards in Key Stage tests and GCSE examinations where there has recently been an increased focus on transference of learning.

After developing his taxonomy, Bloom (1968) and his co-workers went on to explore the most effective conditions for learning. His results are summarised in the graph below. (Fig. 19)

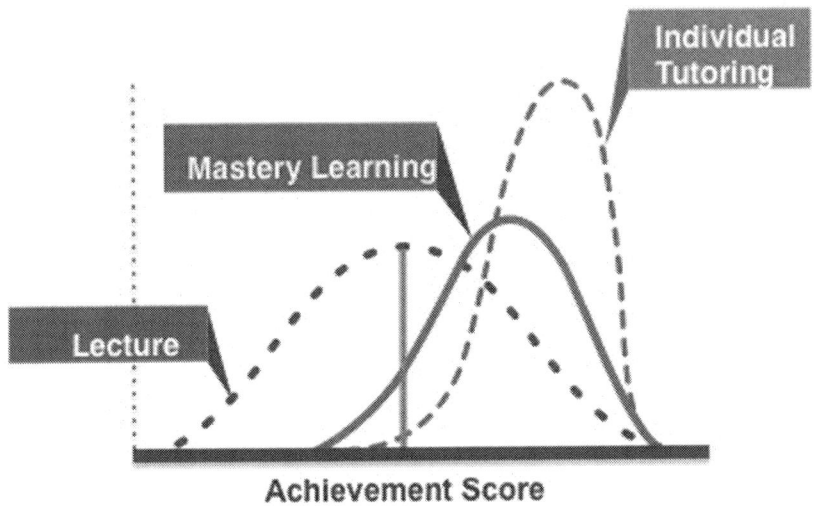

Fig 17. Results of Bloom's research into effective learning. 'The search for methods of group instruction as effective as one to one tutoring' Educational Researcher 1984

Unsurprisingly he found that the most effective arrangement for learning was one-to-one learning situations. He then asked himself which elements of 1:1 learning could be brought into the normal classroom situation. Having decided this, he described this new situation as mastery learning. This is now the basis of many of the learning approaches associated with the new national curriculum. One of the major elements that Bloom suggested to develop mastery learning in the classroom was based on his observation that in one-to-one situations teachers rarely moved on to new learning until the learner had mastered the concept being covered. This was especially important in mathematics and science where learning is sequential and builds on previous understanding. Bloom's mastery learning process is shown below in Figure 18.

Bloom's finding was translated into an approach in mastery learning where the teacher does not move on to new learning until at least 85% of the learners have mastered the learning and that future learning will revisit the topic for those that have not mastered it. Those learners who have mastered a topic go on to work on problems. He called this revisiting of learning 'interleaving'. This interleaving was re-teaching, not a repeat of what happened before. The other observation that Bloom made was that, when learning one-to-one, very few learners (many of them classed as low attainers) failed to reach the average level of learners in a traditional classroom. This is reflected in the much higher expectations of what learners can achieve which we see in the new national curriculum floor targets. Higher-level thinking and problem solving are key to Bloom's concept of mastery learning.

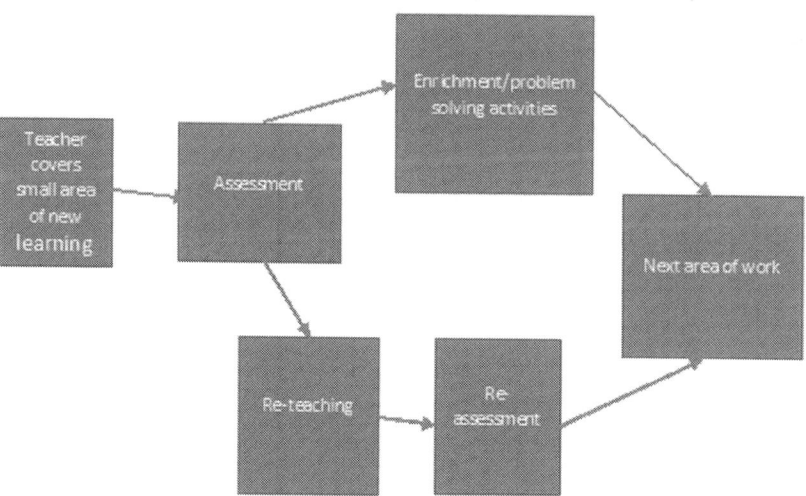

Figure 18. Bloom's Mastery Learning Process

Carol Dweck's (2006) work on Mindset also links with Bloom's higher-level thinking, in that it is essential that learners struggle to learn on occasion, if they are to develop growth mindsets. Higher level thinking activities make this much more likely to happen rather than focussing on the lower levels of knowledge, understanding and applying, where the learner is not involved in such challenging thinking.

Both Bloom's work and that of Carol Dweck was acknowledged in a 2016 paper 'Learning about learning' by the National Council on Teacher Quality. This was a high-level paper produced in America for education publishers, to encourage them to use learning approaches that work.

The following is a summary of their findings.

Learning—What are the six strategies that work?

The first two help students take in new information:

1. Pairing graphics with words. Young or old, all of us receive information through two primary pathways—auditory (for the spoken word) and visual (for the written word and graphic or pictorial representation). Student learning increases when teachers convey new material through both.
2. Linking abstract concepts with concrete representations. Teachers should present tangible examples that illuminate overarching ideas and also explain how the examples and big ideas connect.

The second two ensure that students connect information to deepen their understanding:

3. Posing probing questions. Asking students "why," "how," "what if," and "how do you know" requires them to clarify and link their knowledge of key ideas.

4. Repeatedly alternating problems with their solutions provided and problems that students must solve. Explanations accompanying solved problems help students comprehend underlying principles, taking them beyond the mechanics of problem solving.

The final two help students remember what they learned:

5. Distributing practice. Students should practise material several times after learning it, with each practice or review separated by weeks and even months.
6. Assessing to boost retention. Beyond the value of formative assessment (to help a teacher decide what to teach) and summative assessment (to determine what students have learned), assessments that require students to recall material helps information "stick."

Working in partnership with parents.

For many years, schools have talked about working in partnership with parents, but to what extent this actually happens in practice varies enormously. If you listen in to the sort of conversation that typically takes place at a parents' consultation evening, you rarely hear the language of partnership. It is much more usually characterised by the implicit message 'I am the professional and I am telling you...' Of course, it is true that the teacher is the professional, but this is not the language of partnership and does not acknowledge the huge role parents play in children's learning. We often pay lip service to the fact that a lot of learning takes place outside of school but have not yet begun to see how we can fully utilise this learning in schools.

Some schools and school leaders I have worked with have tackled this issue by trying to establish a common understanding with parents of what learning is and 'what it looks like in this school' as has been covered earlier in the chapter. It is then much easier to engage parents in their child's learning. If, for example, you use Bloom's taxonomy as your model, you can share this with parents so that they begin to understand higher-level thinking and can support the learning more effectively. An example of a resource you could use to do this is the following guide to questions which could be used by parents talking to children about something they have read.

BLOOM'S TAXONOMY—Sample Questions Reading and Writing

Remembering
1. Name all the characters in the story.
2. Write 6 facts from the story.
3. When does the story take place?
4. Where does the story take place?
5. Which character appears first in the story?
6. How does the story end?
7. From what you read in the story, describe what the main character looked like.
8. Using facts you read in the story, describe the setting.

Understanding
1. In your own words, say what the story is about.
2. How did the main character feel at the beginning of the story?
3. How did the main character feel at the end of the story?
4. Think of a main event in the story. Why did it happen?
5. Explain why the story has the title that it does.
6. Draw a picture of a main event in the story.

7. If there is a picture in the story, write what happened BEFORE the picture and write what happened AFTER the picture.

Application

1. Think of a situation that occurred to a person in your story and decide whether you would have done the same thing as s/he did or something different. Write what you might have done.
2. Give some examples of people who have had the same problems or have done the same kind of thing as the person in your story.
3. Select any of the people in the story and think of some things each would do if s/he came to your school during reading.
4. What would you do if you could go to the place where the main character lives?
5. What would the main character do if s/he came to your house to visit?
6. If you had to cook a meal for the characters in the story, what would you cook?
7. If you met the main character in the story on the street, what would you talk about?

Analysis

1. What part of the story was the funniest? Or the most exciting? Or the saddest?
2. Tell what things happened in the story that *couldn't* have happened in real life?
3. Some things in the story were only the opinions of someone. List some of these.
4. Organise the story into parts and think of a good title for each of the parts.

5. What could you do that was just like what the person in the story did?
6. Find 5 words in the story that begin with the same sound.
7. Name 2 things in the story that happened outside (or inside).
8. List at least 5 compound words from the story.

Evaluation
1. Was the main character in the story good or bad? Why?
2. Compare any two books you've read and tell which one you would recommend to your friend/s and why you would.
3. Compare 2 characters in the story. Say which one you think is nicer and why.
4. Which character in the story would you most like to spend the day with? Why?
5. Was this story worth the time it took to read? Why?
6. If you had the opportunity to go where this story takes place, would you want to go?

Creativity
1. Rewrite the story from an animal's point of view.
2. Use your imagination to draw a picture about the story. Then, add one new thing of your own that was not in the story.
3. Make a poster, a mobile, a puppet, or a painting of the main characters in the story.
4. Write another ending to the story that is different from the one that the author wrote.
5. Write a poem about the story.
6. Pretend you are the main character. Write a diary about what you were doing each day.
7. Rewrite the story briefly but change someone or something in it.

8. Write 5 new titles for the story that would give a good idea of what it was about.

Of course, not all parents are as supportive of their children's learning as we might like, but by sharing our thinking about learning we give those who want to support us the chance of helping more effectively.

This is important because we know from the work of Charles Desforges (2003) that parents have a much greater influence on learning than schools throughout primary education and well into secondary school. This research has spurred schools on to try to engage more effectively with parents in terms of their children's learning because of the potential improvement in standards that can be achieved if the efforts of parents and school can be aligned.

In New Zealand they have developed some excellent resources for use by parents who want to support their child's learning. Many aspects of these resources could be used with parents in this country.

Link: http://nzcurriculum.tki.org.nz/National-Standards/Supporting-parents-and-whanau/Resources

Dialogue and Discussion

In his book 'The Fifth Discipline' (1990) Peter Senge says:

> In most organisations, discussion occurs instead of dialogue. Discussion occurs when two or more people state their positions and give the reasons for what they believe. Dialogue occurs when people state their positions, give their reasons, and invite exploration and critique of their reasons and suppositions. Positions are not presented merely for the purpose of defending them. Almost everybody agrees two heads are better than one but act as if my head is better than all of yours combined!

Too often in education dialogue and discussion are confused. Helping to clarify with your team the difference between dialogue and discussion, and when each approach is appropriate, is another way of providing clarity to key communication processes. There will often be situations where, as a leader you are not absolutely sure of the way forward; being able to signal this to your team by asking for a dialogue, and for them to understand what this is, can be a useful tool. This is not a sign of weakness but wisdom! As a leader there will be times when you don't want to have a dialogue because you are certain of the way forward, but at other times a dialogue will be most appropriate.

As a Middle Leader the ongoing dialogue you have with your team and other stakeholders about learning is the most important and must be returned to regularly. We tend to spend far more time thinking about issues related to learning such as those related to assessment and content and not enough on pedagogy. In focussing on this you will help maintain your credibility as a practitioner.

Behaviour for Learning

As we have seen, developing a shared language and model of learning has the potential to engage children more actively in their learning. It also offers the opportunity of making a more concrete link between this shared understanding of learning and behaviour for learning or behaviours that support learning, so that children can understand more clearly the importance of these behaviours. There are many frameworks for behaviour for learning but one of the most useful is the one developed by Costa and Kallick on 'Habits of Mind' (2008). These habits of mind are shown below.

- Persisting
- Thinking and communicating with clarity and precision

- Managing impulsivity
- Gathering data through all senses
- Listening with understanding and empathy
- Creating, imagining, innovating
- Thinking flexibly
- Responding with wonderment and awe
- Thinking about thinking (meta-cognition)
- Taking responsible risks
- Striving for accuracy
- Finding humour
- Questioning and posing problems
- Thinking interdependently
- Applying past knowledge to new situations
- Remaining open to continuous learning

When children are familiar with a model of learning such as Bloom's or Solo taxonomy, it is much easier for them to see the relationship between the sort of learning behaviours shown above, or ones you develop with them, and thus be able to manage their own learning as effectively as possible.

Key points
- Maintain your credibility in terms of learning.
- Model and discuss what good learning looks like.

Further reading:
Collins R, (2014). *Skills for the 21st Century: Teaching higher-order thinking.* Curriculum & Leadership Journal, curriculum.edu.au

Fisher R, (1998). *Thinking about thinking: Developing meta-cognition in children.* Published by Early Child Development and Care, Taylor & Francis

CHAPTER SIX

Building and Managing Your Team

• • •

'A team is not a group of people who work together. A team is a group of people who trust each other.'
Simon Sinek

Another important aspect of your role as a Middle Leader will be building an effective team of people to support you.

There is a large body of knowledge about team effectiveness, so I shall just concentrate on the aspects of the available research that I have experience of using, and which I know has proved useful to leaders in a number of schools. Richard Beckhard is one of the most influential researchers into team effectiveness and he has developed a model to promote this. This is the Beckhard (1972) model for team effectiveness as shown below. (Figure 19)

The model, based on Beckhard's findings about effective teams, is deceptively simple. In essence, it shows that effective teams are clear about their goals, everybody in the team understands the role they need to play in order to reach the goals, people can engage effectively in the processes designed to help to reach the goals and this in turn builds good relationships and the team achieves their goals. He found, however, that the goals need to be articulated in a way that is meaningful to the everyday work of those who are tasked with achieving the goals. If the goals are not clear, then people cannot play a full role in achieving them.

It is easy to fall into the trap of setting a goal without explaining clearly what the goal looks like in terms of the everyday life of the team members who have to deliver it. For example, I once worked with a leader whose stated goal for her team was to promote independent learning. However, when I asked her and the team what they felt independent learning was, there was a debate for an hour and a half! Leaders of teams really need to hammer out what the goals they want to achieve really look like if they are not to confuse the members of a team trying to follow them.

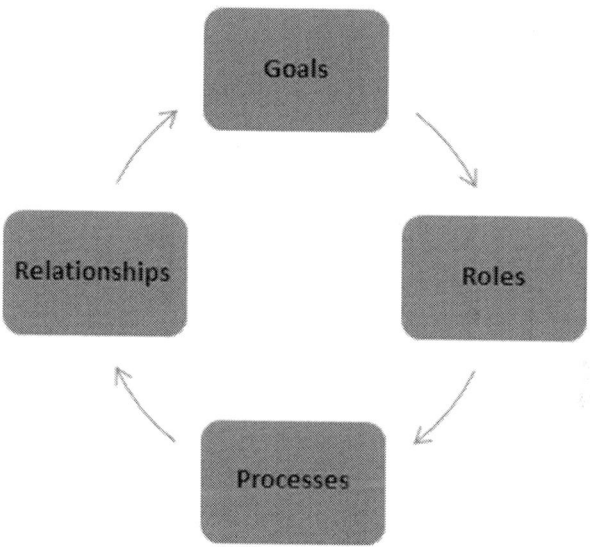

Figure 19. Beckhard Team Effectiveness model

Some interesting follow-up research on the Beckhard model looked at dysfunctionality in teams and found that very often people would describe the dysfunctionality in terms of relationships. 'The problem with my team is Fred! He is always so negative' etc. However, when the dysfunctionality in these teams was actually analysed the relationship issue was often just a symptom of poorly defined goals. If I am a member of a team with poorly defined goals, then I can't play a full role in achieving them because I don't fully understand what we are trying to do. It follows that I then can't play a full part in processes set up to achieve the goals. The frustration that follows from this situation will often impact negatively on relationships. The lesson from Beckhard's work is that all leaders within the school must develop clear, meaningful goals for their teams, covering both the long and short term, if they are to be effective. In many ways you cannot be too explicit when describing goals and what they mean for the way in which people have to work differently in the future, in order to achieve them.

Regularly revisiting the purpose of the team and what you are trying to achieve is also part of establishing the sort of clarity we are talking about. Unless you define the purpose of your team you cannot evaluate how effective you have been! Nonetheless, there are teams meeting in many schools who have never defined their purpose but meet regularly because that is what they have always done.

What do we know about effective teams?

If we look at the observational research on effective teams, we get a list of characteristics like the ones below.

- Have a shared understanding of the vision and tasks that flow from the vision
- The skills of the team meet the needs of the task
- The team members are loyal to each other and respect each other's contribution
- Members work on problems together
- The team adapts and is positive about change
- The team is aware of its development needs
- New members are inducted carefully

- The team takes calculated risks
- The team prioritises and shares leadership
- Communications within the team are good and people can express their opinions
- The team always looks to improve its performance
- The members of the team lead by example

This type of audit is interesting in what it tells us about effective teams but can also provide a useful framework for a team to periodically review its effectiveness. I have used similar lists to help teams reflect on their performance and develop a programme for improved working, since however good they may be as a team, they can always improve.

We also know from the work of Roberts (1990) on highly effective teams that getting feedback on the team's performance is very important. In order to do this effectively, the purpose of the team must be clearly understood by those giving the feedback. If this is not the case the value of any feedback about team performance is obviously greatly reduced. Assuming this is not the scenario, feedback can be gathered simply from members of the team by using the 'what went well, even better if' technique. This method of getting feedback is widely used by NCTL and the language of 'even better if' encourages people to give honest feedback.

The careful induction of new members into a team is often not done well. As well as helping the new member to understand the systems and structures of the team that they have joined, you, as team leader, will also need to help them understand the thinking and developments that the team has undertaken in the last couple of years, so that they have a better idea of the journey the team has taken and the culture of the team. Whenever a new member joins a team, levels of trust fall. This is simply because the dynamic has changed, and members will expect the way the team works to change. This is disruptive in terms of trust levels. Your job as the leader is to re-build the levels of trust as quickly as possible.

Conceptual model of an effective team

One of the observations in the list above is that the skills of the team match its purpose. It is therefore useful to have some sort of framework within which to carry out a skills audit for the team. A number of such frameworks exist, and I have worked with some teams that drew up their own.

Perhaps the most widely used, however, would be the framework developed by Meredith Belbin (1981). Belbin's work led to a conceptual model of an effective team which had the following skill set:

- **Plant**: creative, solves difficult problems. Because their ideas are so novel, they can be impractical at times. They may also be poor communicators and can tend to ignore given parameters and constraints.
- **Co-ordinator**: clarifies goals, promotes decision-making. Their potential weaknesses are that they may delegate away too much personal responsibility and may tend to be manipulative.
- **Monitor-Evaluator**: is a behavioural style associated with analytical, dispassionate, evaluative and critical thinking. Sometimes they are poor motivators who react to events rather than instigating them
- **Implementer**: turns ideas in practical action. On the downside, Implementers may be inflexible and can be somewhat resistant to change.
- **Completer-Finisher**: is good at dealing with the fine detail. However, a Completer-Finisher may worry unnecessarily, and may find it hard to delegate.
- **Resource Investigator**: enthusiastic, explores opportunities.

On the downside, they may lose enthusiasm quickly, and are often overly optimistic.
- **Shaper**: challenges inertia and ineffectiveness. Their potential weaknesses may be that they're argumentative, and that they may offend people's feelings.
- **Teamworker**: co-operative, builds consensus. Their weaknesses may be a tendency to be indecisive, and to maintain uncommitted positions during discussions and decision-making.
- **Specialist**: provides knowledge and skills in rare supply.

As can be seen for each skill set there is an allowable weakness. The weakness is only allowable, however, if the overall skill set in the team is fairly balanced.

(Members of the team can complete a questionnaire which will indicate their strongest skills within the team.)

The first 8 are all skills that are permanently needed but there is also a non-permanent member of the team that Belbin calls the specialist. This extra person was needed because Belbin felt that no team ever had all the specialist knowledge it needed and so at times it would need to work with others from outside the team, in order to get this specialist knowledge. This is interesting when we think of teams in schools, which very often have fixed membership and do not necessarily have a culture of recognising when they need specialist support to help do their work effectively. In some of the most effective Senior Leadership Teams I have worked with they often invite people to join the team and 'Hot Seat' in order to use their expertise. 'Hot Seating', where a specialist comes along and just answers questions is often more effective than inviting them along to give a presentation. 'Hot Seats' have the advantage of ensuring that the process addresses your learning agenda.

There are a number of potential advantages in working with a conceptual model of a team, such as this. If you carry out a skills audit, it helps recognise the leadership skills of all members of the team. If the team leader uses these skills within the team e.g. 'Tim, you are our Shaper—anything we are missing here...?' 'Jane, you are our Plant—any new approaches you can see?' the team can work to its strengths. This also provides a potential way to distribute leadership within the team and grow leadership capacity. The Belbin model can also be used as part of a recruitment process, where identifying a particular skill set is a high priority. The other advantage of carrying out a Belbin skills audit of your team is that it enables you to work more effectively with both your strengths and weaknesses. The Emotional Intelligence link, outlined by Goleman (1998), between self-awareness and self-management which effective individuals display, is equally valid for teams. Thus, for example, if a team finds itself low on Plant then it could bring in someone more creative to help when dealing with an intractable problem that requires some creativity. Alternatively, it could ensure that a member of the team thoroughly researches the options, what others may have done in similar situations etc., and brings this research to the meeting. Thus, compensating strategies can be developed to make the team more effective.

The dynamics within teams can be very complex but there is no doubt that good professional relationships within your team will be key to your success. You need to know and understand your team to achieve this. It is also important to model the kinds of behaviours you want from the rest of the team. Teams which go beyond the usual 'think' and can challenge each other's views, in a non-destructive way, are most likely to have the biggest positive impact on children's learning.

Jim Collins in his book 'How the mighty fall' provides some useful indicators to help judge whether your team is on the way up or down.

Teams on the way down	Teams on the way up
People shield those in power from grim facts, fearful of penalty and criticism or shining light on the harsh realities	People bring forth unpleasant facts to be discussed; leaders never criticise those who bring forth harsh realities
People assert strong opinions without providing data, evidence or a solid argument.	People bring data, evidence, logic and solid arguments to the discussion.
The team leader has a very low questions-to-statements ratio, avoiding critical input and/or allowing sloppy reasoning and unsupported opinion.	The team leader employs a Socratic style, using a high question-to-statements ratio, challenging people, and pushing for penetrating insight.
Team members acquiesce to a decision yet do not unify to make the decision successful, or worse, undermine the decision after the fact.	Team members unify behind a decision once made and work to make the decision succeed, even if the vigorously disagreed with the decision.
Team members seek as much credit as possible for themselves yet do not enjoy the confidence and admiration of their peers.	Each team member credits other people for success yet enjoys the confidence and admiration of his or her peers.
Team members argue to look smart or to improve their own interests rather than argue to find the best answers to support the overall cause.	Team members argue and debate not to improve their personal position, but to find the best answers to support the overall cause.
The team conducts 'autopsies with blame' seeking culprits rather than wisdom.	The team conduct 'autopsies without blame' mining wisdom from painful experiences.

Teams on the way down	Teams on the way up
Team members often fail to deliver exceptional results, and blame other people or outside factors for setbacks, mistakes and failures.	Each team member delivers exceptional results, yet in the event of a setback, each accepts full responsibility and learns from mistakes.

Accountability of teams

Given how much resource is invested in your team it will be important to develop some sort of accountability framework to evaluate how effectively the team has worked together. You could use a simple 'what went well, even better if' approach, or a more elaborate framework similar to the one below, which I have used with a number of teams.

The 10 point health check for teams.

1. What is the team's purpose and is this understood by all who attend team meetings?
2. Does the time spent in meetings match the purpose of the meetings?
3. What is the balance between the time spent solving problems and time spent avoiding problems?
4. What are the responsibilities and accountabilities that go along with membership of the team?
5. What will be different, as a result of the team's work, in 1 year and 3 years from now?
6. How often does the team train together?
7. How does the team get feedback about its performance?
8. How do individual members get feedback about their role in the team?
9. How has the team improved and increased the processes and tools it operates with in the last year?

10. How often do other specialists join the team, in order to help it operate more effectively?

Management of the team.

So far, we have focussed very much on leadership, but all leaders need to be good managers as well. Good management involves having effective and efficient structures and systems in place so that the team does not waste any more time than is necessary in unhelpful bureaucratic activities which do not impact on the key task of improving learning. An important aspect of good management will be effective use of time, and you will need to model this for your team. Good time management, often involves avoiding 'time stealers'.

Looking periodically at how you are managing your time is important as a leader and the time stealers framework below, or some similar tool, can sometimes help you to reflect on this.

	Often	**Some-times**	**Never**
Unexpected and prolonged phone calls			
Colleagues stopping by to chat or discuss their problems			
Open door policy—should be available			
Visitors, not expected			
Poorly trained or incompetent people			
Network meetings that serve little purpose			

	Often	Some-times	Never
Answering and reading non-important emails			
Doing other people's jobs			
Confused and changeable objectives and priorities			
Absence of a daily work plan			
No self-imposed deadlines (or ignoring those you set!)			
Tendency to aim to do too much, perfectionism			
Lack of order, messy desk, poor filing etc			
Confusion and overlap of responsibilities			
Insufficient delegation			
Excessive attention to details			
Delay in dealing with conflicts			
Scattered or too-numerous interests			
Inability to say "no"			
Lack of information, insufficient or excessive communication			
Indecisiveness, or rushed decisions			
Fatigue, tiredness, being unfit and unhealthy			

The reality of leadership is that you will rarely, if ever, have enough time so prioritising the time you have and avoiding time stealers is essential to your effectiveness.

Good Communications

The next area to consider, is how to use the time you do have effectively. Good communications are an essential part of good management and you will need to consider how best to ensure you communicate effectively and then make this a continuing priority for your leadership. This will include giving people prior notice of what will be discussed at meetings, recording decisions and commitments clearly and chairing meetings in a way that ensures your team have a chance to express their views. You will also need to keep to time at meetings! Developing a team handbook can be a useful way to meet some of these needs. Meeting deadlines and commitments is also important and is something that can be made explicit in a short handbook or team folder.

Working Style

There are 5 major working styles that most leaders exhibit. These are shown below. Awareness of our own working style, and its advantages and pitfalls, can increase our range of strategies in order to be effective as leaders. We can identify ways to be more productive and a little self-analysis can unlock major benefits that we may have overlooked. Each of the five major working styles has its own strengths and weaknesses. The weaknesses often result from an overdose of the strengths; we can have too much of a good thing.

When this happens, we stop choosing to behave in a particular way, and start feeling compelled to act in that way. It is as if we are driven by our working style. We feel we have no option, that there is no other way to be that would make sense. For this reason, the working styles are often referred to as our *drivers*.

Whenever we are under stress, we tend to shift from working style into driver mode. We apply our working style so much that we slip into the weaknesses of the style. At the same time, we feel under a compulsion to do this even more; our driver seems to take over. This in turn creates more stress—so we apply our style even more—and create even more stress! This pattern may lead us into a spiralling effect that actually generates more stress, at the same time as we are doing our best to cope. Knowledge of this spiral, and of the working styles, can enable us to take more control over our behaviour and particularly our responses to stress. We can aim to maintain the strengths of our working style whilst avoiding the problems associated with our driver.

Kahler (1975) identifies 5 drivers. These are '*Hurry Up. Be Perfect, Please people, Try Hard and Be Strong*'. Julie Hay (2009) has extended this work to look at the advantages and disadvantages of each working style which are shown below.

1. **Hurry Up**. People with Hurry Up characteristics work quickly, respond well to short deadlines, and get a lot done in a short time. If we are Hurry Up, our motivation is to do things quickly, we feel good if we can complete tasks in the shortest possible time and our energy peaks under pressure. Our major strength is the amount that we can achieve. We spend less time preparing than others do, giving us a chance to meet more people and contribute more to the team. However, this gives us time to spare and we delay starting until the job becomes urgent - then we start work on it. This can backfire because in our haste we make mistakes. Going back to correct the mistakes takes longer than doing the job right first time, so we may miss the deadlines after all. Our ability to think fast makes us appear impatient. We speak fast and have a habit of interrupting others. We may even finish their sentences for them, often misunderstanding and getting involved in needless arguments. Our meetings get planned too close together, so we rush from one to another, arriving late and leaving early.

2. **Be Perfect**. Be Perfect people are as unlike Hurry Ups as can be. Be Perfect characteristics involve a quest for perfection—no errors, everything must be exactly right, first time. This working style means we are well organised because we look ahead, plan for potential problems, do our best to make sure everything will run smoothly. We can be relied on to produce accurate work. Our strengths are our reputation for accuracy, our attention to detail and our thoroughness. Unfortunately, we cannot be relied on to produce work on time because we need to check it so carefully for mistakes and we are reluctant to issue a draft rather than the final version. We are also likely to misjudge the level of detail required. We include too much information and have the effect of confusing the recipient. We choose our words carefully and may therefore use long, less familiar words or technical terms that others do not understand.

3. **Please People**. Please People are the good team members. We encourage harmony, we are intuitive and considerate of others' feelings. Our aim is to please other people without asking. We work out what they would like and then provide it. This working style means we are nice to have around because we are tolerant and understanding. We pay attention to the feelings of those around us and draw the team closer together by ensuring that everyone's views are taken into account. Please People are also nurturing and caring. We show a genuine interest in other people at a personal level. We are encouraging and reassuring when other people have potentially stressful tasks to undertake. Unfortunately, we can be too nice! In our efforts to maintain good relationships we may fail to speak out. We let other people implement ideas that we know are likely to fail— but we don't say anything in case they 'take it personally'. Then we are hurt

when they get angry with us for not warning them. We may also become so anxious about retaining the approval of others that we seem almost paranoid about remaining pleasant at all costs. We are the ones who apologise when someone steps on our foot.

4. **Try Hard**. The Try Hard working style is all about the effort put into the task, so we tackle things enthusiastically. Our energy peaks with something new to do and we like to follow up on all possibilities. This results in a thorough job in the sense of paying attention to all aspects of the task. People value our motivation and the way we have of getting things off the ground. Managers appreciate the fact that we often volunteer to take on new tasks. However, we may be more committed to trying than to succeeding. Our initial interest wears off before we finish the task. Our attention to so many aspects makes the job impossibly large, and even if we complete most of it, we may still think up yet another angle to pursue before we can really agree that the job is done.

5. **Be Strong**. Be Strong people are calm under pressure, good at dealing with stress, great to have around in a crisis. With this working style, we feel energised when we have to cope. We have a strong sense of duty and will work steadily even at the unpleasant tasks. We will also keep on thinking logically when others may be panicking. Because we are so good at staying calm and dealing with all that the job throws at us, we are seen as consistently reliable, steady workers. Our problem with this style is that we hate admitting weakness—and we regard any failure to cope as a weakness. So, we get overloaded rather than asking others for help. We may disguise our difficulties by "hiding" work away; often our desk looks tidy but correspondence is filed away in a rather large pending tray. We may also find that other staff feel uncom-

fortable about our lack of emotional responses in situations where most people tend to feel the strain. It may be hard to get to know us when we seem to have no feeling.

In thinking about how to best manage our own working style it is also useful to reflect on the working styles of members of our team and how we can work most effectively with them.
What to look for:
- **Hurry Up**: Their speech pattern is to speak quickly, using phrases like "Let's get on with it".
- **Be Perfect**: They use words like "obviously" and "as I was saying", and they speak slowly and deliberately, often using "brackets" to give extra information.
- **Please People**: They use phrases like "You know" and "sort of".
- **Try Hard**: They use the word "try" a great deal.
- **Be Strong**: They de-personalise their thoughts in their speech patterns by using passive language: "It seems that" rather than "I think".

When working with people with a particular working style the following advice is useful in helping them avoid going into driver mode:
- Hurry Ups get praised for being quick so set out to get recognition for accuracy as well.
- Be Perfects get praised for accuracy, look for recognition for meeting deadlines and appropriate levels of detail.
- Everybody thinks Please People are nice, aim for recognition for being assertive.
- Try Hard people score points for enthusiasm, get recognition for finishing tasks—successfully.
- Be Strong people often get low key recognition for not needing help; watch how relationships improve when you let people help you.

Knowing the work style of members of your team is an important part of getting to know them and working effectively with them.

Key Points
- Get to know the members of your team and use their strengths.
- Model the team behaviours you want.
- Always define goals and vision in a way that helps people understand what they need to do differently and thus their role.

Further reading:
Lencioni, Patrick. *The Five Dysfunctions of a Team*, 2002, John Wiley & Sons ISBN: 978-0-7879-6075-9

CHAPTER SEVEN

Developing Trust and Motivating Staff

• • •

'Really great people make you feel that you, too, can be great'
Mark Twain

In your reflections and readings on leadership you will find the importance of developing trust within your team is highlighted in much of the research.

Trust, however, in not easy to define although I think the quote that 'trust is what happens when values and behaviours match up' is both useful in clarifying what we mean by trust and helpful in trying to achieve it. Leaders who are personally effective are often ones in whom followers express high levels of trust. Building trust is a key element in achieving success as a leader. However, there is always tension for a leader between levels of monitoring and levels of trust and getting the balance right is never easy. Covey and Merrill (2006) in their book 'The speed of trust' look at leadership behaviours that help to build trust. These are shown in the list below and are a good starting point in terms of how to begin to build and maintain trust in your team.

- Talk Straight
- Demonstrate Respect
- Create Transparency
- Right Wrongs

- Show Loyalty
- Always look to improve
- Practise Accountability
- Listen First
- Keep Commitments, and
- Extend Trust
- Confront Reality
- Clarify Expectations

The other interesting aspect of Covey and Merrill's findings is that organisations where levels of trust are low are very inefficient because so much time and effort is spent checking things. Thus, you should always be trying to grow trust in your team, in order to make the team more efficient and effective. Covey and Merrill do not advocate ever relinquishing the need to monitor as a leader, merely that you need a balanced approach and the direction of travel should be towards greater trust and less monitoring.

Levels of trust within a team are dynamic and sometimes you will need to make building trust more of a priority in terms of your time. This can be especially important at times of rapid change. Indeed, at these times a leader builds trust and cohesiveness simply by keeping people informed. Having in mind some indicators of levels of trust is useful when making judgements about where the team is in this respect Examples of such indicators are the number of staff asking questions and contributing at team meetings, the level of risk taking in the team, even the body language of the staff and the use of humour.

As we have mentioned before, as a Middle Leader there can be some tension between your role in terms of maintaining quality control of the work the team is doing and maintaining levels of trust. The equation:

High levels of monitoring = Low levels of trust

is a good summary of this potential tension. If this is a problem in the context you find yourself working in, then being explicit with your team about this issue will be the first step to solving it.

It is also important to remember that trust and motivation are intrinsically linked. Team members find it more congenial to work in a high trust environment, and this has a very positive effect on their motivation.

Some aspects of motivation, however, are very personal and what motivates one team member may not always motivate another. This is yet another reason to get to know team members well as individuals. However, there is useful research about what teachers generally value, a summary of which is shown below.

- Participation in decision making
- Use of valued skills
- Freedom and independence
- Challenge
- Expression of creativity
- Opportunity for learning

Many of the Middle Leadership tools and behaviours we have looked at chime with this list and will help you to motivate members of your team. You should also not neglect your own motivation. Sometimes leaders can be so busy worrying about their team's needs they forget about their own. Always remember the beliefs and vision that led you to be a leader and ensure that you continue to do things you enjoy and that motivate you.

Key messages
- Leadership behaviours are key to building trust.
- Successful motivation strategies are personalised.

Further reading:
Maslow A (1943). *A theory of Human motivation*. Psychological Review
Herzberg, Frederick (1966). *Work and the Nature of Man*. Cleveland: World Publishing. OCLC 243610.
Whitaker T, Whitaker B and Lumpa D, *Motivating & Inspiring Teachers: The Educational Leader's Guide for Building Staff Moral*. Routledge (2008) ISBN-10: 1596671033

Chapter Eight
Networking
• • •

'If you want to go fast, go alone. If you want to go far go with others.'
African proverb

Networking is possibly one of the most important skills for leaders in today's new education landscape. Networking involves building and maintaining contacts and relationships with other people, both from within and outside of the school you work in. The most important aspect of networking is that it provides opportunities for *learning*. As schools begin to collaborate more and more within Academy chains, Trusts and Federations, as well as the more traditional Local Authority clusters, the challenge of staying in touch with developments in learning becomes more challenging. The education system is now less centralised, and there are many advantages to this, but it also means that it is more difficult to keep your finger on the 'pulse of change'. Middle Leaders need to find, join or form networks that help them do this. These networks will be based both on subject specialisms but also school leadership. In the past these sort of networks were often built up over time as you moved through your career. Nowadays, it is essential that leaders make forming networks a priority and become proactive in doing so.

For many years now Headteachers have had a number of network opportunities but these have been more limited for Middle

Leaders. Increasingly, however, Headteachers are seeing the value in facilitating networking for their Middle Leaders and you should use your influence to encourage this. You should also be an advocate for networking for members of your team.

Providing time for networking can be problematic but the use of technology such as SKYPE or Webex can be used to mitigate some of the problems. The benefits of networking are as follows:

- Provides the opportunity for benchmarking your professional experience with that of others.
- Provides an opportunity to hear about other approaches to shared issues.
- Has the potential to build links between similar teams in different schools.
- Helps to build confidence through discussion and narrative learning.
- Helps to keep you up to date with policy changes etc. that relate to your role.
- Provides an opportunity for targeted CPD

Not all networks of course achieve these things and some unfortunately often become focussed on problems rather than solutions. You will need to ensure you choose wisely which networks to support with your time.

Increasingly some of the most useful networks are on social media. There are now thousands of education blogs, from those of HMI to class teachers, and some of these are very useful sources of new thinking.

Top Tips for Successful Networking

In terms of how to network effectively, which can seem a rather nebulous subject, I think the top tips shown below, developed by Southampton University, provide very thorough advice.

1. Have a purpose
   Think about what you want to achieve from networking. Networking is much more productive and enjoyable when you have a clear goal in mind.
2. Be proactive
   Even if you currently receive requests to meet or connect with others, simply waiting for people to contact you will only give you a fraction of the benefits that reaching out to new or existing contacts can offer. Setting yourself a stretching, but achievable **target** can be a helpful way of making sure you remain proactive. An example of a relevant target might be 'I will attend two networking events next month'.
3. Take a varied approach
   Engaging in both online and face-to-face networking can often be more effective than using only one of these approaches. It is good practice to build a varied network. This doesn't mean connecting with as many people as possible but building relationships with people in other **relevant contexts**. Having a broad network can help you build your knowledge base.
4. Join a professional networking site e.g. teacherstalk.co.uk
5. Attend relevant events
   The networking events you attend should be appropriate to your personal aims and/or your profession/role. Conduct some research in advance; if your colleagues or friends have been to an event you're interested in, ask them for some feedback. It is also a good idea to find out who else is attending the event you have in mind, as this can give you a good indication of whether or not it is relevant. Ask the organiser for an attendance list.

6. Perfect your introduction
   One of the most important ways to ensure you feel confident about speaking to others at networking events is to prepare a brief, engaging introduction. This does not mean writing a 'script' as such but having a comfortable grasp of what you want to say when you first introduce yourself. Your introduction should be fairly brief and should convey key pieces of information about you in a positive and interesting way.
7. Ask engaging questions
   To establish rapport with someone new, it is important to ask some well-considered questions once you have introduced yourself. The purpose of this isn't to interrogate the other person, but to find out more about them and spark a more in-depth conversation. Depending on your reasons for networking, and the purpose of the event you're attending, you may wish to ask the other person about their role and responsibilities, their professional background, and why they were first drawn to the event.
8. Follow up with people you meet
   When you meet someone new at a networking, it is important to exchange contact details so you can stay in touch. It is good practice to send the other person a brief email the next day or invite them to connect with you. If there is something specific you wish to discuss with a new contact after meeting them at an event (e.g. a potential collaboration or new venture), you may also wish to schedule a phone call or arrange a meeting.
9. Network internally as well as externally
   It is just as necessary to build relationships within your school as it is to do so with external parties. Offering to coach and mentor would be one way of doing this.

10. Stay in touch with your network

    Maintaining your existing network is just as important, if not more so, than growing it. If you haven't been in touch with some of your contacts recently why not send them a brief email or arrange a meeting to catch up? Nurturing these relationships will help to ensure they remain effective and beneficial over time.

    When it comes to staying in touch with your network, though, it is important to strike the right balance and leave an appropriate amount of time between each interaction with your contacts. Remember that people are busy and may not always have a chance to come back to you immediately. If you send an email or leave a message for someone and it isn't urgent, give them a few days to respond before trying them again.

11. Help others

    It is important to add value to your network, as well as derive value from it. If someone asks you for help, advice or guidance, try to assist them if you can, or put them in touch with someone else who can help. You might also be able to offer your knowledge and expertise by contributing to relevant discussions on professional networking sites. Depending on your contacts and their needs, you might also be able to introduce people to one another or share relevant articles or pieces of research with them.

12. Say thank you

    If a member of your network has helped you in any way, it is important to acknowledge this and thank them for their assistance. Sending an email or note can often be an effective way of doing this.

13. Be trustworthy

    Trust is vital in any relationship. Never share confidential information you hear through networking unless you have permission to do so; if you're not sure whether a piece of information is confidential, keep it to yourself until you have.

14. It's about quality, not quantity

    When you are connected to more people than you can stay in touch with, the quality of your network and its potential to help you achieve your objectives is likely to suffer. To keep things under control, make sure you only engage in relevant networking activities, and ensure your online network is populated with people you know and trust.

15. Share your expertise

    If you are already a strong networker, you will have a lot of skills and expertise that some of your less experienced colleagues might be able to benefit from. If you know someone who is struggling with networking, why not offer to provide them with some advice, or even informal coaching? If you are interested in sharing your expertise on a larger scale, you could offer to facilitate a training session on networking for the rest of your team.

16. Learn from your experiences

    As you network more actively, it is good practice to reflect on the lessons you learn along the way: what works well for you and what might you need to improve? These insights will help you to refine your approach to networking and ensure it continues to be successful and effective.

In very small schools, where staff tend to be very close in terms of relationships and staff turnover can be slow, networking is especially important.

Key points
- Be proactive. Find, join, form networks.
- Encourage your team to network effectively.

Further reading:
Mackay, Harvey. *Dig your well before you're thirsty*, 1997. Bantam Doubleday Dell Publishing Group, ISBN-10: 0385485468

Chapter Nine
Next Steps in Leadership
• • •

'It is not what happens to you that determines how far you go in life; it is what you do with what happens to you.'
Zig Ziglar

On your journey to Middle Leadership you may have been given, and taken, opportunities offered to you, in order to extend your leadership experience. In travelling on from Middle Leadership it will be helpful if you have continued to do this. Indeed, you may have been proactive in making this happen by volunteering to take on tasks and extra responsibilities. Middle Leaders who offer solutions rather than problems are always welcomed by Senior Management!

You can also take the initiative in investigating areas in which you know you will require a greater level of understanding for the next step in your career. One example of this might be in the area of the financial management of the school. As a Middle Leader you may well have been responsible for a budget for your area of responsibility but typically this will be small in terms of the overall budget for the school. For Primary schools the average overall school budget is now close to £1 million and for secondary schools several millions. Thus, understanding effective management of resources is a key leadership skill. In order to see the bigger picture in terms of school finance, it might be worth making time to talk to the school business manager or finance officer and getting to grips with how the school budget is generated and allocated. Understanding, for example, that for every unfilled school place, over a five-year period, can cost the school on average £20,000, helps to begin to see the full picture in terms of school finance and the importance of reaching capacity in terms of pupil numbers. School finances have a direct impact on learning and so developing an understanding of how they work is a real priority for school leaders.

The other area where you might seek some added experience is working with governors. As a Middle Leader you may well be linked with a particular governor, as is often the case in schools nowadays. This relationship can be useful in terms of finding out a bit more about the wider role of governors and their responsibilities. However, if you actually volunteer to be a governor, perhaps at another local school, this will give you a real insight into the relationship between governing bodies and school leaders.

Changes to the educational landscape which we mentioned earlier have had a big impact on school governance and many new and different models of governance are emerging. Being proactive in learning about the effects of these changes will be very useful in moving into senior leadership in the future.

Another aspect of your personal effectiveness that you can work on in preparation for moving into a senior leadership role is developing resilience. Anybody who has worked in education understands the tremendous sense of achievement working with children engenders. However, they also know teaching is not an easy job and this is even more true of school leadership! Therefore, developing resilience as a leader is important.

Building Resilience

Resilience is often described as a personal quality that predisposes individuals to bounce back after setbacks. In education this is an essential quality to try to develop as a leader. Given the very high levels of accountability that exist in education, together with the increasing number of difficult situations school leaders now have to deal with, developing high levels of resilience has become essential.

As a Middle Leader you also need to monitor signals of flagging resilience within your team.

Indicators include:
- the team fails to keep learning.
- people blame everything on the budget or some other problem outside their control.
- leaders and team members ignore critical indicators.
- too many initiatives drain people.
- success goes uncelebrated.

As individuals there are strategies that have proved useful in building resilience. These include:
- don't forget to do things you enjoy.
- stay hopeful.
- choose your words carefully to create a positive climate.
- don't become defensive when something goes wrong.
- cultivate networks.
- use other people's insights and strengths.

Given the undoubted number of issues facing school leaders it may seem difficult to stay positive and hopeful, but it is absolutely essential. If, as Middle Leader, you are talking negatively about something the Headteacher or SLT have introduced, your team will read into this that you don't support it and therefore they have no need to. You are also modelling a behaviour they may choose to repeat when you introduce something they don't like. These situations are delicate because you don't want to diminish your authenticity by supporting something you are not in favour of. A good strategy is to avoid making a judgemental comment about the change or policy you have doubts about and just outline your understanding of why the decision or change was made. Assuming the Headteacher or SLT are rational there will be reasons they took the decision even if you would not have come to the same conclusion. Loyalty demands that you share their thinking with the team.

Being hopeful and helpful as leader is also important in establishing a solution-focussed approach within your team rather than a problem-focussed approach. The following analysis shows the characteristics of each.

Solution-focused versus problem-focused thinking in the workplace

Activity	Problem-focused	Solution-focused
Planning change	Emphasis on diagnosis 'Can you tell me about the problem?' Identify all the blocks to change	Emphasis on desired outcome Identify progress already made Highlight strengths and resources
Managing people	Sees people as sources of dysfunction Who is the weak link? How can we minimise the risk people represent?	Sees people as functional and sources of solutions. Where are the hidden strengths? How can we grow our people?

Activity	Problem-focused	Solution-focused
Monitoring progress	Emphasis on identifying weaknesses and failures 'What went wrong last week?' Record and react to undesirables. Look how far we have yet to go.	Emphasis on identifying what works and gains made. 'How did you cope so well last week?' 'What is different about those times when it works well?' Look at how far we have come.
Trouble shooting	Emphasis on explaining problems. Uncover the cause and effect chain. 'Is lack of progress a symptom of something deeper?'	Emphasis on improving progress and identifying doable goals 'What else might help?' 'Have we identified the right goal?' How do others overcome this? What other ways can it be done?

Sometimes it's the small things that count most!

In concluding what I hope you have found to be a useful, practical guide to successful Middle Leadership, I would just like to share one other observation I have made about successful leaders. Sometimes it is not the big things you do that have the biggest impact. Malcolm Gladwell (2000) makes the same point in his book 'The Tipping Point'. I can think of examples of this from my own Headship. When I started as a Head I decided that at each assembly I would read out the names of three pupils and ask them to bring all their books the next day so that we could discuss their work.

This had a far greater effect on standards than I could ever have imagined. Of course, it was not a panacea, but it did tighten marking and assessment and increased motivation for a lot of pupils. I have seen similar things happen in other schools when working with Headteachers. One Head changed all the signs within the school which read 'Children' to 'Learners'. When you walked around that school this really made an impression and was an effective statement about their priorities and beliefs. The moral is really to remember that you don't have to make major changes at once and not to overlook the small things that can be put right and lead to incremental and sometimes large improvements.

Finally, professional learning is key to success in leadership as we have already said. Preparing for your next role by following a National Leadership programme such as NPQSL or NPQH would give you an overview of school leadership which would prove invaluable in your career and I would encourage you to become involved in these should the opportunity arise.

In my experience leaders relish taking on new roles but sometimes after a number of years, when they feel less challenged, this level of motivation is harder to maintain. When you feel like this, it is probably time to move on with your career. Good luck and I have included a reading list to help you on your way!

Key messages.
- Leaders must be helpful and hopeful.
- Leaders must model the behaviours they want from their followers.

Appendix 1

• • •

Leadership reading list

Collins J, *Good to Great*, Harper Business 2001 ISBN:9780066620992

Covey S. R., *The Seven Habits of Highly Effective People* 1989 ISBN 0-671-70863-5.

Covey S. R., *The 8th Habit: From Effectiveness to Greatness* 2012 ISBN-10: 1455893064

Covey, S. R., *Principle-centred leadership.* New York : Fireside 1990 ISBN-10: 145589348X

Drucker P. *The essential Drucker.* Harper Business 2001 ISBN-10: 0066210879

Fullen, M, *The moral imperative of School Leadership* 2003 ISBN-10: 0761938737

Fullen, M *Leading in a culture of Change* 2001 ISBN-10: 0787987662

Gladwell M, *The tipping Point,* Publisher: Little Brown 2000 ISBN 0-316-31696-2

Goleman, D, *Working with Emotional Intelligence.* New York: Bantam Books 1998 ISBN 0553104624

Goleman D *Social Intelligence* Arrow 2006 ISBN-10: 0099464926

Hattie, J *Visible Learning for teachers* Routledge 2008 ISBN-10: 0415476186

Kline, Nancy *Time to think.* Cassell 2012 ISBN-10: 0706377451

Scott S, *Fierce Conversations,* Publisher Judy Piatkuss 2002 ISBN 0670031240

Senek, S, *Start with why* Penguin 2011 ISBN-10: 0241958229

Shirley, L, Hord, M and William A. Sommers *Leading Professional Learning Communities: Voices from Research and Practice* Corwin 2007 ISBN-10: 1412944775

Senge P, *The fifth discipline,* Doubleday/Currency 1990 ISBN 0385260946

Inspiring leadership videos

https://www.youtube.com/watch?v=wQPCM40fb-s

https://www.ted.com/talks/benjamin_zander_on_music_and_passion

https://www.ted.com/talks/simon_sinek_how_great_leaders_inspire_action

https://www.ted.com/talks/ken_robinson_says_schools_kill_creativity

https://www.ted.com/talks/margaret_heffernan_why_it_s_time_to_forget_the_pecking_order_at_work

https://www.thersa.org/discover/videos/event-videos/2013/07/how-to-help-every-child-fulfil-their-potential-

https://www.ted.com/talks/bill_gates_teachers_need_real_feedback

https://www.youtube.com/watch?v=H0hPqsOVacE

https://ed.ted.com/on/IgslePtt

https://www.ted.com/talks/roselinde_torres_what_it_takes_to_be_a_great_leader/reading-list?ga_source=embed&ga_medium=embed&ga_campaign=embedT

References

Anderson, L. W., Krathwohl, D. R., Airasian, P. W., Cruikshank, K. A., Mayer, R. E., Pintrich, P. R., Raths, J., Wittrock, M. C. (2000). *A Taxonomy for Learning, Teaching, and Assessing: A revision of Bloom's Taxonomy of Educational Objectives.* New York: Pearson, Allyn & Bacon. ISBN-10: 080131903X

Beckhard, R, (1969). *Organization Development: Strategies and Models*, Addison-Wesley, Reading. ISBN-10: 0201004488

Beckhard R, (1972). *Optimising Team Building Efforts*, Journal of Contemporary Business

Belbin M, (1981). *Management Teams*, London; Heinemann. ISBN 0470271728.

Biggs J., Collis, K. (1982) *Evaluating the Quality of Learning: the SOLO taxonomy.* New York: Academic Press ISBN-10: 0120975521

Blank S, (2013) *The Four Steps to the Epiphany: Successful Strategies for Products That Win*, K & S Ranch ISBN-10: 0989200507

Bloom B (1956). *Taxonomy of Educational Objectives, Handbook I: The Cognitive Domain.* New York: David McKay Co Inc. ISBN-10: 0582280109

Bloom, B. (1968). *Learning for Mastery. Instruction and Curriculum.* Regional Education Laboratory for the Carolinas and Virginia, Topical Papers and Reprints.

Burns J M, (1978). *Leadership.* NY Harper and Row. ISBN-10: 006196557X

CfBT publications (2010). *Coaching for teaching and learning: a practical guide for schools.*

Collins J, (2001). *Good to Great.* Harper Business ISBN: 9780066620992

Collins J, (2009) *How the Mighty Fall: And Why Some Companies Never Give In*, Random House Business ISBN-10: 1847940420

Cooperrider D, Srivastva S, (1987) *Research in Organisational Change and Development.* Volume 1 pp 129-169, JAI press

Costa A, 'Learning and Leading with Habits of Mind: 16 Essential Characteristics for Success', 2008. Association for Supervision & Curriculum Development. ISBN-10: 1416607412

Covey S. R. (1989). *The Seven Habits of Highly Effective People.* Free Press. ISBN 0-671-70863-5.

Covey, S. R., (1990). *Principle-centered leadership.* New York : Fireside ISBN-10: 145589348X

Covey S (Junior), Merrill R, (2006.) *The Speed of Trust : The One Thing that Changes Everything,* Simon & Schuster Adult Publishing Group ISBN-13: 9780743297301

Desforges C, Aboucaar A. (2003) The impact of parental involvement, parental support and family education on pupil achievement adjustment: a review of the literature DFE publication Queen's Printer. ISBN 1 84185 999 0

Dudley, P, (2014). *Lesson Study: A handbook,* www.lessonstudy.co.uk

Dweck, C. (2006). *Mindset: The new psychology of success.* New York: Random House. ISBN-10: 0345472322

General Teaching Council of Scotland (2016) *The Standards for Leadership and Management – Middle Leaders,* http://www.gtcs.org.uk/web/FILES/professional-development/selfeval-sa-slm-middle-leaders.pdf

Gibbs, G. (1988) *Learning by Doing: A Guide to Teaching and Learning Methods.* Oxford: Oxford Further Education Unit

Gladwell M, (2000). *The tipping Point*, Publisher: Little Brown ISBN 0-316-31696-2

Goleman, D, (1998) *Working with Emotional Intelligence.* New York: Bantam Books ISBN-10: 0553378589

Goleman D, Boyatzis R, McKee A, (2004) *Primal Leadership* HBS Press ISBN: 1591391849

Goleman D, (2001) *Leadership that gets results*, Harvard Business Review

Goleman D, (2003) *The New Leaders: Transforming the Art of Leadership*, ISBN-10: 0751533815

Hattie, J, (2008). *Visible Learning: A Synthesis of Over 800 Meta-Analyses Relating to Achievement.* NY: Routledge. ISBN 978-0-415-47618-8.

Hay J, (2009). *Transactional Analysis for Trainers*, Sherwood Publishing, ISBN-10: 1907037004

Ishikawa, Kaoru (1968). *Guide to Quality Control.* Tokyo: JUSE.

Joyce B, Showers B, (1988). *Student Achievement Through Staff Development: Fundamentals of School Renewal.* Longman. ISBN-10: 0871206749

Joyce B and Showers B, (1996). *The Evolution of Peer Coaching. Educational Leadership.*

Lewin K, (1951). *Field Theory in Social Science*: Selected Theoretical Papers. Harper & Row

National Council on Teacher Quality, (2016), *Learning about learning*

Pentland A, (2015), *Social Physics: How Social Networks can make us smarter*, Penguin ISBN-10: 0143126334

Scott S, (2002). *Fierce Conversations*. Publisher Judy Piatkuss ISBN 0670031240

Senge P, (1990). *The fifth discipline*, Doubleday/Currency. ISBN 0385260946

Southworth G, (2005). *The essentials of school leadership*. Sage Publications Ltd

Sutton Trust, (2011), *Improving the impact of teachers on pupil achievement in the UK – interim findings*

Whitmore Sir J, (1984.) *Coaching for Performance*. Publisher Nicholas Brealey ISBN 1857883039

Printed in Great Britain
by Amazon